UNLOCKING
YOUR
LEGACY

UNLOCKING YOUR LEGACY

25
KEYS FOR
SUCCESS

PAUL J. MEYER

MOODY PUBLISHERS
CHICAGO

ISBN: 0-8024-1787-6

1 3 5 7 9 10 8 6 4 2

Printed in the United States of America

ENDORSEMENTS FOR *UNLOCKING YOUR LEGACY*

"One of America's greatest entrepreneurs reflects on what you will carry across the finish line. Paul Meyer has written the Cliff Notes for how a successful businessman can lead a Christ-directed life. Highly recommended."

> Patrick Morley, men's author and President of Man in the Mirror

"Paul Meyer is among the few who are truly qualified to teach on the subject of legacy because he genuinely lives his legacy every day. This book is practical and leads to legacy-building action. Give your best to your family and friends; start reading this life-manual today!"

> William Nix, President of the WorkLife Company, Author of *Character Works* and *Transforming Your Workplace for Christ*

"Paul J. Meyer is the 21st century 'guru' for personal development for mind and spirit. His books and materials for self-help efforts have recently reached their highest pinnacle for helping people reach their highest potential. *Unlocking Your Legacy* is his greatest work to date, and I predict it will make a mark for good and God in your life that cannot be erased for all eternity. This is a 'must-read' book, and it will produce a 'must-be-blessed' to every reader. Every layman who goes to work every morning will gain a new insight for his job when he reads Paul's concept in his chapter 'My Work Is My Ministry.' Read this book today, and you will thank Paul for his efforts . . . just like I did."

> Gil A. Stricklin, Founder & President of Marketplace Ministries, Inc., Dallas, Texas

"It is my privilege to recommend Paul Meyer's most recent book, *Unlocking Your Legacy*. This work is a treasure trove of foundational Christian insights organized around the theme of legacy, but involving some of the most fundamental questions about life. Paul's words about the stewardship of life, commitment to Christ, the use of one's gifts, discipline, and so many other themes make this book a manual for Christian living."

> Robert B. Sloan Jr., President of Baylor University

AUTHOR BIO

Paul J. Meyer is considered by many to be the founder of the personal development industry. The combined sales of his printed and recorded materials are more than two billion dollars worldwide, more than any other author in this field, dead or alive. Though he claims he officially retired at age 70, he maintains his lifetime goal of doing all the good he can, to as many as he can, for as long as he can. He is also the co-author of The New York Times best-seller, *Chicken Soup for the Golden Soul.*

To my wife Jane
> —*you are the most balanced person on earth and the joy of my life!*
> *My legacy is your legacy.*

To my children Jim, Larry, Billy, Janna, and Leslie
> —*you make this dad proud!*

To my grandchildren Mike, Brady, Cole, Allison, Jason, Jessica, Jennifer, Joshua, Adam, Christie, Morgan, Brooke, Kelsey, and Jordan
> —*I look forward to your future!*

To my parents, August Carl Meyer (1892–1963) and Isabelle Rutherford Meyer (1892–1969)
> —*your legacy lives on!*

To my sister Elizabeth (1926–99) and brother Carl
> —*hardly a day goes by that I don't reflect on the times we enjoyed together.*

And to everyone I have ever met or will meet through these pages
> —*your legacy is of your making, unlimited, and able to change the world!*

CONTENTS

FOREWORD
BY JOHN C. MAXWELL

L et me take this opportunity to express my highest regard for Paul J. Meyer and for what he stands for. He has made an enormous impact in my life and I will always be grateful for that.

I first heard of Paul in 1970. I was a young man, just out of seminary and recently married, still finding my feet as a new pastor. I was invited to a presentation on how to set and achieve goals, hosted by a company I had never heard of before, Success Motivation Institute, Inc.

Looking back, it was as if that night I traded in my chuck wagon for a bullet train. My eyes were opened to the reality of living in the world of the "impossible," setting goals, and taking giant steps toward my destiny. I was so impressed that I knew I needed to immerse myself in the principles outlined in Paul's course, but the cost was more than I could afford at the time. I immediately went home and asked my wife Margaret what we could cut out of our budget so I could buy the course.

We bought the course and it profoundly affected my ministry and my career for Christ. I often think of that crucial night and am grateful for the effort that Paul went through to write out those principles and to make them available for everyone.

A few years ago I had the opportunity to have dinner with Paul and his wife Jane at a restaurant in southern California. One of the first things I said was, "You never let your hero pay for dinner." He asked what I meant and I explained the impact he had made on my life. He was touched, and so was I.

For decades I have used his materials, either for myself or for leaders across the nations, and am always amazed at the changes that take place in people's lives. But I should know better—everything Paul puts his hands to is life-changing!

I see *Unlocking Your Legacy* as the condensed version of everything that Paul has believed, practiced, and taught for more than fifty years. In addition, he is one of those rare individuals who actually does what he says he will do! In fact, he keeps track of his promises and puts them in a vault and then at the end of the year incorporates them into his will! His word is as good as gold—*even better!*

He has taken seriously the fact that "a good man leaves an inheritance for his children's children" (Proverbs 13:22) and understands that this means much more than just a financial inheritance. He is the first to point out that every area of life is vitally important and has its respective legacy.

As you read Paul's wisdom, advice, and personal stories, keep in mind that he has already done what he is talking about. *He isn't talking theory—he's talking reality!*

The fact is, everyone will leave a legacy, but few take any action to positively affect their legacy. Some may go so far as to map out a course for leaving a legacy, but only a handful of those will actually walk the road themselves. Even a smaller number will return and give the map to those who come after. *Paul J. Meyer is one such man!*

Regardless of any limitation we might place on ourselves, we have an incredible opportunity to learn from someone who has charted a course before us. Take it and run!

Paul, it is a joy and an honor to write these words of appreciation and recommendation. You are more than qualified to write this book and I have no doubt that *Unlocking Your Legacy* will motivate thousands of readers to leave a legacy that others could only dream about.

Thank you again for playing a part in unlocking my legacy those many years ago.

Admiringly,

John C. Maxwell

INTRODUCTION
WHERE A LEGACY BEGINS

I t was in Lindach, Germany, on the steps of a church my family had attended for over 200 years that the realization hit me—*I am leaving a legacy behind!*

The church, built in 1505, had witnessed the marriages and burials of my own family members, not to mention all the wars and cultural changes experienced during the last 500 years! Being aware that so much of my family's history had taken place right where I was standing sent chills up my spine and brought tears to my eyes.

> EVERYONE LEAVES A LEGACY, WHETHER IT IS INTENTIONAL OR NOT. THOSE WHO ARE MORE INTENTIONAL ABOUT IT USUALLY LEAVE A BETTER LEGACY BEHIND.

It was an interesting combination of emotions, but I knew then that I needed to record for future generations the principles that had impacted my life.

With a keen sense of gratefulness, I considered my own history. My father left Germany just before World War I and arrived in New York after a harrowing journey on a ship that was lost at sea for almost two months! He worked and saved money, eventually making it to the land of his dreams: California.

He ended up doing carpentry work for a man whose wife had an eligible sister visiting from Michigan. Within months my father and Isabelle Rutherford were married, resulting a few years later in three children, the youngest of which was me.

WHAT IF...?

Countless things could have happened from that time until this. I separate these very real "What if...?" possibilities into two categories: accidents and decisions.

Accidents:
"What if my father didn't have a short leg and had been forced to fight in WWI?" or "What if my parents had never met?" or "What if, at age 16, the car I was driving in a rainstorm had hydroplaned off the cliff instead of toward the mountainside?"

Decisions:
"What if I had reacted differently after being fired from a job?" or "What if I had decided to pursue another career?" or "What if I hadn't listened to my instincts?" or "What if I had never moved to Texas?"

Considering every "What if...?" possibility makes it obvious that none of us truly control our own destiny. I am always quick to give God credit for His hand in my life. Scripture says,

"I am the LORD your God, who teaches you what is best for you, who directs you in the way you should go" (Isaiah 48:17). It's a good thing too! If it weren't for Him directing my steps on a daily basis, there is no telling what my legacy would be.

WHAT IS A LEGACY?

In its most basic sense, a legacy is something handed down from one generation to the next, such as a sum of money or a piece of property. But a legacy is not restricted to money. It also includes traits, habits, talents, and attitudes that are social, physical, mental, spiritual, and emotional. *In essence, everything you are and possess today, whether good or bad, is your legacy.* This is what will pass down to those who come after you.

Because a legacy can come in many forms, I divided my legacy into several categories. For me, a good legacy should:

> EVERYTHING YOU ARE AND POSSESS TODAY, WHETHER GOOD OR BAD, WILL PASS DOWN TO THOSE WHO COME AFTER YOU.

A) be based on godly principles

B) produce lasting results

C) be applicable to everyone

D) work in all six areas of life

   1. financial & career

   2. family & home

   3. spiritual & ethical

   4. social & cultural

   5. physical & health

   6. mental & educational

If it is worth instilling in my legacy, it will fit within these parameters.

WHAT IS A LEGACY KEY?

I see a legacy like a safe-deposit box that is filled with all sorts of valuables. It is only natural that the owner of a safety deposit box would tell the recipient what is in it, how everything works, and why it is so important—and then turn over the key.

> **A GOOD LEGACY ISN'T FREE AND CERTAINLY ISN'T INSTANT.**

For this reason, the following chapters are divided into Legacy Keys, each containing a principle that will unlock a portion of one's legacy. I've put these principles into practice for more than fifty years—and they work!

But regardless of what may be in the safe-deposit box, *it is up to the recipient to choose what he or she will do with the key* and *the valuables inside*. All responsibility, however, does not rest on the shoulders of the one receiving the legacy—the one giving it is equally responsible.

What is the secret to making this a success? There is only one way: through active participation. This process is just like our children going to kindergarten. They move up to middle school, to high school, and then to college. Each is a step toward growing up that we admittedly cannot take for them. They walk it out for themselves, and by doing so, they benefit the most from the experience.

The same applies to our legacy, which is why *leaving a legacy takes time* and why *receiving a legacy requires effort*.

GOOD LEGACY—BAD LEGACY?

Like my father, someday my legacy will also be my history, so until that day comes I am doing everything within my power to leave behind a good legacy. But in all my efforts, I've come to understand that *a good legacy isn't free and certainly isn't instant.* It will require that you give up your money, your time, and yourself.

A bad legacy, on the other hand, requires no concerted effort for attainment. Do nothing different and a son or daughter will receive exactly what the parent left behind. Like water always flowing downhill, so a bad legacy will pass effortlessly from one generation to the next.

It is important to note that every legacy has both good and bad in it. To deal with this reality, each of us must have the discernment to choose what we want to pass on to the next generation. For example, my father left me a great legacy, but it included the terrible trait of unforgiveness. Choosing to be a forgiving person and not including this dreadful habit in my legacy did not diminish the good legacy I received.

HOW WILL LEAVING A LEGACY AFFECT WHAT YOU DO?

When we realize that we are leaving a legacy behind, our perspective changes radically. I once heard of a church that was built around A.D. 1000. When it came time to replace the aging roof some 200 years later, the original construction plans were brought out and studied. There in the plans was a detailed note explaining where a forest had been planted at the time of the church's construction consisting of a specific type of tree that ought to be used for the roof's support beams.

> IF WE DO NOT MAKE PLANS FOR A BETTER TOMORROW, TOMORROW WILL BE NO BETTER.

The trees were discovered exactly where the plans stated— *having been planted in neat rows 200 years earlier!* Only someone with a long-term mentality could have ever thought of planting a forest for a need that did not yet exist!

To operate with such a mentality, our perspective must change. What's more, our heart, mind, body, and soul must undergo a change as well. The fact is, if we do not make plans for a better tomorrow, tomorrow will be no better.

A long-time friend of mine, though now deceased, came to this revelation early in life. He was an illegitimate child who grew up on the streets. He worked his way through college on the GI bill and eventually got married. He stayed married and reared a family.

He told me one day, "Much of what I do is a conscious decision—it doesn't come naturally because I never experienced it myself. What my children have today is the result of me choosing *not* to live the life that my parents left me."

It is amazing that a man who had so little good in his legacy (he didn't even know who his father was!) could turn around and leave such a rich heritage to those who came after him.

I believe it was the result of two decisions he made: first, committing his life to Jesus Christ and walking in the wisdom and healing that only God can give, and second, making a conscious decision to instill certain principles into his children's lives.

Today, each of his children has a personal relationship with Christ and is doing tremendously well. For the legacy he received and the legacy he left behind to be so different, radi-

> THE ONLY BOUNDARY ON YOUR LEGACY IS THE BOUNDARY YOU PLACE ON IT YOURSELF.

cal changes were required. He willingly accepted every change because he understood that passing on a good legacy requires a long-term mentality.

Each of us must do the same.

THREE MAIN REASONS WHY I WROTE THIS BOOK

First, I wrote this book to encourage you to focus on what is truly most important in life. With so many distractions, it is little wonder that we need to continually refocus our attention, time, and money on the things that are of highest value and importance. Like the apostle Paul, I have purposed that I will someday say, "I have fought the good fight, I have finished the race, I have kept the faith" (2 Timothy 4:7).

It is my hope that the principles within these pages will enable you—and those who come after you—to do the same.

Second, I wrote it for those who never had a good legacy, much less a Legacy Key passed down to them. It doesn't seem fair that some would inherit so much, while others would inherit so little, but we all begin where we are.

- ◆ If we received an empty wallet, we are the ones to fill it.

- ◆ If we were the first to accept Christ as Lord in our family chain, we need not be the last.

- ◆ If we experienced negativism and "I can't," we can pass on positivism and "I can."

- ◆ If we grew up as perpetual victims, we can break tradition and be a generation of victors.

- ◆ If we came from a home of broken promises and failure, we can choose to pass on a legacy of honesty and success.

Whatever your history, tomorrow is *your* future. This book is for you because *your future can be absolutely anything you want it to be!*

Third, and last, I wrote this book for my children and grandchildren as well as for every associate, employee, friend, and acquaintance I have had over the years. I wrote it for everyone I have ever met.

How I have lived my life has and will impact their lives. It is my hope, wish, desire, and prayer that those coming after me will be both encouraged and equipped to continue where I left off and to excel beyond their highest expectations in every area of their lives!

I took the good legacy I was given and added to it. Now I pass it on to you.

- - - - - -

In my mind I can see myself standing in front of that old church in Germany. I still feel the emotions, the tears of appreciation and thankfulness, and the chill down my back.

I have a legacy that I will someday leave behind.

And so do you.

PART ONE

WHERE EVERY GOOD LEGACY BEGINS

LOVE—
WHERE EVERY GOOD LEGACY BEGINS

—BECAUSE EVERYTHING OF VALUE MUST START SOMEWHERE

When I was a boy, I saw love in action and learned quickly that it came in many different forms.

- My brother, Carl, loved me by the way he fought off three bullies when I was just 15 years old and small for my age.

- My sister, Elizabeth, loved me by always having a listening ear and a kind word for me.

- My father loved me by the way he trained me, disciplined me, and spent time with me.

- My mother loved me by demonstrating how to forgive, how to communicate, and how to know God.

- My teachers loved me by giving me a lot of their time.

Having love around me, however, did not make life perfect. I had plenty of hurts and disappointments, not to mention many setbacks and losses, but in the midst of the realities of life, love always seemed to blossom. That is because love cannot be held captive by our thoughts, emotions, fears, or outside limitations.

Love brings unstoppable freedom when we learn to love as God intended.

> LOVE BRINGS UNSTOPPABLE FREEDOM WHEN WE LEARN TO LOVE AS GOD INTENDED.

THE GREATEST COMMANDMENTS OF ALL TIME

Jesus said there was no greater commandment than to "love the LORD your God with all your heart, with all your soul, with all your mind, and with all your strength" and to "love your neighbor as yourself" (Mark 12:30–31 NKJV).

Then, as if that wasn't enough, Jesus later added, "A new commandment I give to you, that you love one another; as I have loved you, that you also love one another" (John 13:34 NKJV). That changes things considerably!

Loving God may seem easy enough (He never treats us badly and always has good things in store for us) and loving others like ourselves may seem doable, but loving others as Jesus loved us?

Here is a sampling of the ways Jesus showed His love for us:

◆ He stopped to talk with the lowest of the low.

◆ He dispensed justice wherever He went.

◆ He healed the social outcasts.

◆ He ate with sinners.

◆ He cared for the poor.

◆ He gave up His will.

◆ He allowed His body to be beaten for our sake.

◆ He died on the cross for our sins while we were still sinners.

Loving others to the extent that He loved us is impossible, but that is the point! *We cannot do it on our own—we need Him!* And unless we have His love in our hearts, there is no way we can love others wholly, purely, or adequately.

That makes sense only because "God is love. Whoever lives in love lives in God, and God in him" (1 John 4:16). Without God, there is no love, but if we have Him in our hearts, then it is possible to give and demonstrate His love.

WHAT EXACTLY IS LOVE?

God is love, but what are the characteristics of love that we need to see evident in our lives? First Corinthians 13:4–8 NKJV plainly states, "Love suffers long and is kind; love does not envy; love does not parade itself, is not puffed up; does not behave rudely, does not seek its own, is not provoked, thinks no evil; does not rejoice in iniquity, but rejoices in the truth; bears all things, believes all things, hopes all things, endures all things. Love never fails."

> "HOW CAN YOU LOVE IF YOU DON'T HAVE LOVE IN YOUR HEART?"
> —The Seventy Sevens

That is love.

I once loaned money to the very company that fired me. My own desires wanted other things for them, but I chose to show Christ's love, regardless of how I had been treated. The $10,000 I loaned them to stabilize their company did in fact bring the stabilization they needed, so much so that a few years later they sold the company for 8 million dollars!

My act of love was of no financial benefit to me, but that was not the point behind my actions. I was motivated to love as Christ commanded—that was all.

How we practically show God's love comes in many different forms. My mother, for example, was like a magnet. Her love for others drew people to her like children to free ice cream. When my sister was young, she and her friends would come home and hang out with my mom. Most moms were not "cool" enough, but my mom loved those girls so much that they couldn't help but gravitate toward her. On top of that, her counsel was always timely and her presence seemed to soothe away their fears. The positive impact she had over the years through her love cannot be measured!

> **LOVE IS LONG-TERM THINKING. ALL ELSE IS SHORT-TERM, IF EVEN THAT.**

Love also comes in the form of discipline. My dad gave me plenty of that—and I love him for it. Scripture says, "The LORD disciplines those he loves, as a father the son he delights in" (Proverbs 3:12). If my dad had not disciplined me, I would not be the man I am today.

Sacrifice is also love in action. I have friends who sacrificially give of their time, talents, and money to charities that are helping the homeless, the hungry, and the poor. When asked why they have given for years without as much as a "thank you," I have seen them begin to cry and say, "I am doing so little. There is so much more that I could do."

The love so evident in their lives is the very love that Jesus commanded us to give. Our love, He said, should focus in three different directions: toward God, toward ourselves, and toward others. Each one is of utmost importance.

#1

WHAT DOES IT MEAN TO "LOVE GOD"?

We are commanded repeatedly in Scripture to love God with our heart, mind, body, and soul. Practically speaking, this simply means that we are to obey Him in every area of life, for "if anyone obeys his word, God's love is truly made complete in him" (1 John 2:5).

This does not leave much room for loving other things, but that is part of God's plan. He wants us to focus on Him and to love Him exclusively. If we love God with everything within us, He has an amazing way of pouring back into us more than enough love for other people. That is because He doesn't just sit back and receive our love. Instead, He reaches out to us, touching our lives and blessing us.

Here are just a few of His promises:

> ◆ *Eye has not seen, nor ear heard, nor have entered into the heart of man the things which God has prepared for those who love Him.*
> —1 Corinthians 2:9 NKJV

> ◆ *For God has not given us a spirit of fear, but of power and of love and of a sound mind.*
> —2 Timothy 1:7 NKJV

> ◆ *And we know that all things work together for good to those who love God, to those who are the called according to His purpose.*
> —Romans 8:28 NKJV

> ◆ *Neither death nor life, nor angels nor principalities nor powers, nor things present nor things to come, nor height nor depth, nor any other created thing, shall be able to separate us from the love of God which is in Christ Jesus our Lord.*
> —Romans 8:38–39 NKJV

Though we love God through our obedience to Him, we always come out better off. (Somehow that doesn't surprise me.)

> **HOW CAN WE LOVE LIKE JESUS LOVED?**
> **THE TASK IS OVERWHELMING ON PURPOSE.**

WHAT DOES IT MEAN TO "LOVE YOURSELF"?

Loving God and accepting that He loves you is the foundation for loving yourself, for self-confidence, and for self-esteem.

Loving self is therefore not the same as being self-centered or egotistic.

I have always believed that I have every right to succeed. This view does not cause me to believe that the world owes me anything. In fact, since I officially retired at age seventy, I'm just as active as I was before; it's just that now I have more freedom in choosing what I want to do with my time.

Work is something I will always do, and though I believe I will succeed, I act wisely and do the necessary preparation and planning to hit my goals. *This belief in myself is love for self in action.* The world can be cruel at times, as can close confidants, but I cannot let that get in my way. I must believe in myself before I believe in others.

This type of confidence in self gives you confidence to see others succeed. Their phenomenal growth doesn't discourage you in the slightest because you believe you have the same potential—if not more!

The "everybody owes me" attitude in our society is partly the result of no love for self. After all, love includes self-discipline, taking responsibility, and the realization that we have a part to play in our own success. If we succeed with no foundation (i.e., a foundation of integrity or self-discipline), the fall back to reality will hurt worse than if we had fallen from our prior lowly condition.

That is why most lottery winners are almost always worse off a few short years after winning the jackpot. They had no foundation before and they had no foundation after.

> IF WE DON'T LOVE OURSELVES, WE CAN'T LOVE OTHER PEOPLE.

Love for self, on the other hand, prepares us for greatness.

#3
WHAT DOES IT MEAN TO "LOVE YOUR NEIGHBOR"?

The foundation for loving our neighbor is comprised of two parts: a proper love of self and a desire to love others as Christ loved us. And since a "neighbor" is every person, regardless of race, gender, or age, we get to love everyone!

I've made it a habit to show love to people by noticing them, listening to them, asking them questions, and discovering their interests. Then, through a series of circumstances, I've ended up hiring many of them! In fact, some of the best individuals I've ever had working for me have come as a result of my simply showing interest and love.

I also make it a point to always be real, show respect, treat them as I would like to be treated, focus on their strengths, and try to be an encouragement to them. What happens as a result is often amazing.

One time I was in a restaurant with a friend when I happened to ask the waitress what she wanted to do with her life. She briefly told me she had always dreamed of going to college, then walked away. A few minutes later, the waitress and her mother (who worked in the kitchen) showed up and begged me to take the two of them out of town! The mother's domineering husband owned the restaurant, the mother explained, and she and her daughter were trapped and wanted out.

> "ANGER IS A SIGN THAT WE ARE ALIVE AND WELL. HATE IS A SIGN THAT WE ARE SICK AND NEED TO BE HEALED."
> —Lewis B. Smedes, *Forgive & Forget*

There was no way I could fulfill their request, but by me showing a little bit of genuine kindness, two individuals I had spoken with for only ten minutes in my entire life were begging me for help! A little love can make an unexpectedly big impact.

I once met an elderly man who was offering some prime

property for sale. A few days later I returned to buy it, but by asking a few additional questions, I discovered that the real owners of the property had gone back on their word and were refusing to give him the commission he rightly deserved.

I immediately called the owner and said the deal was off unless he agreed to pay the commission, which he reluctantly agreed to do. The $25,000 commission came at a good time for the elderly man and his wife because they had no savings for retirement. I instantly made a friend that day by simply treating someone like I would like to be treated.

WHY GOD COMMANDS US TO LOVE OTHER PEOPLE

We all have had people rip us off, hurt us, and abuse us in other ways. Agreeing not to retaliate is good, *but God is asking us to go even further and to love them!* Why?

I believe there are three reasons:

1. For our own benefit

2. For their benefit

3. For God's benefit

#1—FOR OUR BENEFIT

From God's perspective, I believe He is more interested in our personal growth and character development than He is in what we do or how we look. Scripture says, "Man looks at the outward appearance, but the LORD looks at the heart" (1 Samuel 16:7).

When we love others, we are demonstrating that we are obeying God and placing our desires second to His—a sure sign of character development.

> IN WHATEVER WAY WE SHOW OUR LOVE FOR GOD, *IT IS FOR OUR BENEFIT!*

And when others do not love us, we have the chance to show what is really in our hearts, as Matthew 5:46 NKJV says,

"For if you love those who love you, what reward have you? Do not even the tax collectors do the same?"

Tax collectors in Jesus' day were the lowest of the low, selfish scoundrels who collected taxes (plus a little bit more) from their own people for the Roman government. If we love only those who love us, our actions are no different than those who were considered to be the worst of society.

By loving those who don't love us in return, we are showing that we are different, controlled by something stronger than our own naturally selfish desires—*it shows the love of God at work in our lives.*

I remember my mother when I think of this type of love. If people hurt her, her level of love would only increase. I was amazed time and time again to see the love that poured out of her. By choosing to love others as Christ loved her, my mother was full of joy, peace, strength, hope, laughter, and a lot more. It is this kind of legacy that I have a strong passion to pass on to my children and grandchildren, to all who are associated with me, and to everyone I meet.

In addition, when we show love through our actions, God will reward us, just as Scripture says, "But love your enemies, do good to them, and lend to them without expecting to get anything back. Then your reward will be great, and you will be sons of the Most High" (Luke 6:35).

#2—FOR THEIR BENEFIT

Obviously, those who have hurt you benefit by your not repaying them as they rightly deserve, but above and beyond that, they benefit by meeting Jesus through your love.

Several years ago a professional person in my town confronted me in his office with a damaging yet completely false accusation. I tried in vain to communicate the actual facts, but he would hear none of it. The conversation hurt me so badly that my health was severely affected.

As I was recovering, I decided that I would pray for him

and do all I could to help him in his personal life. Instead of mentioning this individual's actions to other professional people who might know him or meet him, I chose to forgive him (forgiveness and love always go together). Two years later he called me and admitted he was wrong. When he asked for my forgiveness, I was quick to give it and was very relieved to have dealt with the issue.

"Love will cover a multitude of sins" (1 Peter 4:8 NKJV) and knows no limits. Showing the love that Jesus intended will pave the way for others to know the same love, *which is the greatest benefit of all!*

#3—FOR GOD'S BENEFIT

I believe that by loving others like Christ loved us, we are able to accomplish His purposes in our individual lives. In essence, when we are obedient, He accomplishes His will. That is definitely to His benefit.

However, His greatest desire by far is that every individual comes to know Him as his or her Lord and Savior. Scripture says, "God so loved the world that he gave his one and only Son, that whoever believes in him shall not perish but have eternal life" (John 3:16). He paid the costliest of prices for us, showing us the "full extent of his love" (John 13:1).

Over the years I have hired many individuals who were down on their luck. They needed another chance to prove themselves. I offered it to them and was glad I did. Several went on to great careers, some moved on to another job, while a few went back to their old bad habits.

Many of those who took advantage of the opportunity of a second start have since come back to me and asked questions

> "LOVE IS AN ACT OF THE WILL, NOT THE EXERCISE OF EMOTIONS. TRUE LOVE INVOLVES THE TOTALITY OF ONE'S BEING. GOD, AND ONLY HE, EXPRESSES IT PERFECTLY."
> —John Edmund Haggai

about my faith and my relationship to God.

That, I believe, is how God benefits through our acts of love. After all, "it is not the will of your Father who is in heaven that one of these little ones should perish" (Matthew 18:14 NKJV). God paid an extreme price for each one of us, so when we through our love bring a person to know Him, the greatest benefit is God's.

THE REALITY OF LOVING OTHERS

Love that is given away might not be returned—*this is a fact of life!* Jesus commanded us to love, but He did not say we would be loved in return. I do believe, however, that we always, someway, somewhere, somehow, someday reap what we sow, even in the area of love. However, *it is impractical to demand love from those we have loved.* Loving is simply part of our service to others.

I don't pin my expectations on whether or not people appreciate what I do or not. I've shown kindness to some people, only to be ridiculed the moment I walk away, but what do I expect? I move on.

We cannot think that everyone will love us in return. We need to learn to live with that type of rejection, recognizing that we have been primarily and most importantly obedient to God and His Word. We can then walk in peace, *which makes what others say or do completely irrelevant!*

First John 3:16 NKJV requires our serious attention: "By this we know love, because He laid down His life for us. And we also ought to lay down our lives for the brethren."

To be honest, loving others in this way is a continual process, and though it will take time and effort, it is absolutely the best place for every legacy to begin.

WE ALL STAND ON LEVEL GROUND

—THE IMPORTANCE OF SEEING OTHERS EYE TO EYE

Whoever heard of being raised with no prejudice, no color lines, no socio-economic lines, no position lines, no gender lines, and no educational lines? Is that even possible? I would doubt it, except for the fact that I was the one raised this way.

My parents taught me that everyone stood on level ground, and from that one truth many other principles were driven into my formative heart and mind. Being first-generation German immigrants to the United States, they were forced to learn how to adapt to the society around them.

But instead of being timid and taking only what they were given, they set out to establish themselves in every way they could. A "you can't do that" meant they would not stop until they had accomplished what could not be done. They were not rebellious, but they were fighters, willing to invest themselves 100 percent into a project to see it completed. This I-will-not-be-denied attitude permeated every part of their lives and overflowed into my life as well.

When it comes to people, I have found that the same principle applies.

WE ARE ALL CREATED EQUAL

A teacher once said, "Everyone is equal." In the back of the room a discouraged young man spoke up, "Yeah, but some people are created *more* equal than others."

What did he mean by "more equal"? Technically it is impossible to have degrees of equality because something is either equal or it isn't, but he was implying that life was not fair and that he did not feel he was getting what he rightly deserved.

Well, the truth of the matter is that life is not fair, and the sooner we figure that out the better. *However, this does not mean we don't have a fighting chance to get what we feel we are being denied!*

> A FORMATIVE MIND HAS NOTHING TO DO WITH AGE AND EVERYTHING TO DO WITH ATTITUDE.

For example, in my first job search I applied to fifty-seven different companies and was denied by every single one of them! They denied me because I did not have a college education. They were heavily prejudiced and highly opinionated, and without asking what I could do, how motivated I was, how much common sense I had, or anything about my work ethic, they all said, "No thanks."

Life did *not* seem fair! But instead of quitting, I kept trying. I finally got a job—selling insurance to black families out in the country. It was the only job the company would let me have because they considered it to be the lowest job possible.

I jumped at the opportunity because my dad had always said, "Never take a higher position without first being an apprentice." This was a great opportunity to be an apprentice, and I have always considered myself fortunate because I had that opportunity. What I learned was invaluable, as were the wonderful people I met.

But the companies that discredited me did a
themselves. I went on to out-perform every salesr
on and won every sales competition I entered. The way ...
every company lost that did not give me an equal chance.

Similarly, if we discredit a person, without giving him or
her a fair chance, we lose as well. We must retrain our hearts
and minds to see people as they ought to be seen. After all,
there was a time when we were young, inexperienced, and
denied for some unexplainable reason ourselves.

During the Gulf War, with Iraq still occupying Kuwait, I
heard of two foreign students studying in England. One was
from Kuwait and the other from Iraq. They were best of
friends, even though their countries were at war. If one had
said, "You are an enemy of my people; I cannot befriend you!"
they both would have missed out. Instead, they decided for
themselves what they would do and not do.

Such an attitude is sorely needed in every people group
today.

THE CENTER OF YOUR WORLD

Have you ever
noticed how differ-
ent countries print
world maps? In North
America, the center
of the map contains
North America. In
Europe, Europe is the
center. In fact, I've
even seen maps where

3 WAYS TO SEE EYE TO EYE
1) CONSIDER THE NUMERICAL ODDS OF BEING BORN WHO YOU WERE
2) REALIZE SOMEONE ELSE KNOWS MORE THAN YOU DO
3) THINK OF OTHERS THE WAY YOU WANT THEM TO THINK OF YOU

New Zealand and Australia are in the center *and* on top of the
world! The caption on the inverted map reads, "No longer
down under."

It is only natural for a country to see itself as the center of the world, since national pride is to be expected, but the truth of the matter is the world does not rotate around one nation or people.

I have traveled extensively and have noted, especially in Asian countries, that I stand out like a sore thumb. It's hard to blend in with everyone else when you are tall, white, and fair-haired. The experience has always been good for me and I highly recommend it for others.

Several years ago I was in China with my wife Jane, our daughter Leslie who was about ten years old, and a few close friends. Leslie has blue eyes and at the time had very blonde hair. Because it was the early 1980s, few Chinese had seen— much less met—a child with blonde hair and blue eyes. As a result, complete strangers would walk up and touch her hair.

She was shocked and grew increasingly nervous, refusing to go out in public the following day. Only with Mom's encouragement and the cover of a stocking cap would she venture into the streets again.

There are only a few countries, not counting Europe, where Leslie could travel and not instantly be identified as a foreigner. Some people get tired of being visible, watched, and recognized and almost wish they could swap skin colors so they would blend in. When you think like that, you begin to see the people around you in a different light. *You could just have easily been born in a different country under a different name—with a very different future!*

Linda Wittig, a teacher and nanny for the three grandchildren of a successful Japanese businessman, once admitted to me, "My parents became a lot wiser *after* I became a foster parent and was on their side of the coin." When her experiences changed, so did the way she saw her parents.

Whether people are rich or poor, powerful or weak, seeing them from *their* perspective will do wonders for your relationship. I've spoken with wealthy businessmen, famous dignitaries, former Presidents of the United States, foreign ambassadors, college students, single parents, school teachers, teenagers, preachers, and more. They all have their own set of needs and wants, but I can talk to them eye to eye because I have learned to see what is important to them.

DON'T LOOK UP—AND DON'T LOOK DOWN

Always trying to stay on level ground, my parents taught me to keep my eyes fixed straight ahead. That way I wouldn't think too highly of some (as if they can do no wrong) or too lowly of others (as if they can do no right). Neither approach is correct. The lowest paid person deserves the same respect as the highest paid person.

> YOU COULD JUST HAVE EASILY BEEN BORN IN A DIFFERENT COUNTRY UNDER A DIFFERENT NAME—WITH A VERY DIFFERENT FUTURE!

A medical doctor friend of mine, Winn Henderson, once told me that he has had more than 160 different jobs. From washing windows to performing brain surgery, he has done it all, but he says, "I was just as proud doing the menial job as the 'respected' one because all honest work is valuable." Having such an attitude is especially good when it applies to people.

Treating everyone as equals, however, doesn't fit well with some people, especially when it comes to skin color. When I was eighteen years old, I happened to go into a restaurant in Georgia that had a U-shaped counter with a wire screen in the middle dividing the "coloreds" from the "whites."

When the waiter came to take my order, I asked, "What color are the people in the kitchen?" He said they were all black, so I said, "Well, don't you feel a little foolish eating the same food with the same forks and same plates cooked by the same cooks?" I got a lot of glares, but being the inquisitive guy that I am, I just had to ask.

While in the military, which had its fill of disrespect and demeaning of people, my eyes were opened to the "real world."

I had grown up around Italians, Hispanics, Japanese, Germans and others. I thought nothing of it, but apparently others did. One of my best friends when I was young happened to be an American of Japanese descent, so when WWII started, he and his whole family were interned. He had never done anything to deserve such treatment.

When I found he was being forced to move, I went to his house and gave him my most prized possession: my new bicycle I had spent months saving money to buy. It was my way of saying, "The system is wrong, but I believe in you. You are my friend."

> **DON'T LET SOMEONE ELSE'S ATTITUDE INHIBIT YOU FROM GETTING WHAT IS RIGHTFULLY YOURS!**

That experience helped reinforce in me the desire to treat others as they deserved to be treated. When I couldn't change the abuse that was taking place, I could make sure I never did the same when I was in the position of authority. That is the beauty of the I-will-not-be-denied attitude. If you want something, go get it, whether it's personal, mental, financial, or relational. Don't let someone else's attitude inhibit you from getting what is rightfully yours!

It comes down to choices, whether we want to believe something we've learned or not. Fortunately for me, what I was taught was also what is correct—*that we all stand on level ground.* That is one reason why I have always been able to call on anyone, anywhere, anyplace, at anytime, with a fearless attitude and belief that I will never be rejected. I believe that the welcome mat is always out for me. Why not, since I always have the welcome mat out for others!

Incorporating this belief system into your daily life, then training those who come after you to do the same, is one of the greatest ways of showing you truly believe that everyone is created equal. Imagine what the world would be like if we lived out the belief that we all stand on level ground!

TELLING OTHERS ABOUT YOUR FAITH

—FINDING THE RIGHT
WORDS IS EASY WHEN
YOU USE YOUR OWN

Several years ago, after more than three decades of doing business in Japan and speaking in every major city to tens of thousands of business executives, I was given a unique opportunity. My friend and associate Hei Arita asked me to speak from my heart to over two thousand executives about what living my life according to Christ's principles really meant to me.

I usually don't get tense before giving speeches, but that night I was. I even had a back spasm to prove it! Saying what I was going to say had never been done before in the history of our company. I wondered how the audience would react, but with all the daring and boldness I had within me, I walked down the aisle from the back of the room and onto the platform.

For the next twenty minutes, as I spoke honestly and openly from my heart in a loving manner, the words seemed to roll off my tongue. I had prayed that God would use me, but I didn't know to what degree He would answer my prayer. When the meeting was over, 287 Japanese executives came forward to accept Christ and more than that number, I heard later, became open to Christianity!

I don't remember a word I said that night, but I do know that I was real, 100 percent me. Perhaps that was part of what made my words palatable to those men whose culture and background were so different from mine. All I did was talk about my life and how God made it meaningful.

JUST BE YOURSELF

> **THE BEST INVESTMENT I EVER MADE?**
>
> WITHOUT A DOUBT: TAKING JESUS UP ON HIS OFFER.

At age sixteen, when I asked Jesus into my heart, I really didn't know the ins and outs of being a Christian. I did know that if it meant being religious—following rituals with little or no personal relationship with Jesus Christ—then I wasn't into it. But the more I learned about God's love and His plan for my life, the more I realized that He was both real and relevant.

Always being an investment-oriented individual, it didn't take me long to see the incredible deal I was getting. God's one-of-a-kind offering (of salvation, forgiveness, peace, joy, eternity in heaven, and more) couldn't be found anywhere else; and what it would cost me (giving my heart and life to Him) *was insignificant in comparison to what I got in return!*

I made that investment with joy and expectation—and I've never been disappointed.

Those business executives sitting in front of me that day in Japan were wise investors as well; otherwise they wouldn't have been in the businesses they were in. And so, heart to heart, I gave those men the same investment tip that I had first been given many years earlier by my mother. They had the right to make the same investment and receive the same return on their investment as I did—and many accepted Christ's offer. Since that time, several thousand of our sales associates and their clients have followed suit.

Does leading people to Christ make me an evangelist? I never would have thought of myself as such. I was merely being myself and telling others of how fortunate I was to have found the best investment of all. I do know that we cannot all be what are traditionally called "evangelists," but we are all to "do the work of an evangelist" (2 Timothy 4:5).

The secret is to be yourself. If you think like an investor, then talk like an investor. If you are a painter, then use paint, if an author, then use written words. Because we are all so different, I don't recommend using a "six-easy-steps-to-salvation" approach with people. However, I am quick to acknowledge that using tracts and other more structured forms of witnessing are effective with some people. Neither approach feels right to me, but they might for someone else—so I wish them success.

> **THE SECRET . . . IS TO BE YOURSELF.**

I do know what works for me and that is what I focus on. In *Gentle Persuasion*, author Joseph C. Aldrich explained, "Your talents are the clue to where you fit in the process of evangelism." Each of us has a role to play and we are simply to use the gifts we have to help draw others into the kingdom of God.

Problems arise, however, when we try to be something or somebody we are not, especially in the area of telling others about our faith.

PERFECTION NOT REQUIRED

Before you can share your faith with those around you, *it is **not** a prerequisite that you be perfect*. However, obedience is required. We cannot knowingly disobey the Word of God and expect to benefit or to help other people.

I once bought some quality tools from an employee who was "sad to part with them" but was willing to because he needed the money. Soon afterward a friend informed me that my "new" tools already had my initials on them—because they were my tools to begin with! This was the latest in a string of incidents with this double-crossing employee, so I let him go (he effectively fired himself). *How could he knowingly do what was wrong and expect to benefit from it?*

So it is in our relationship with God. We cannot continue to do our own thing when He is telling us that we need to change. If He pinpoints an area, like cheating, neglecting our family, or poor stewardship, then we need to obey by repenting and changing. If He demanded perfection, none of us would measure up, "for all have sinned and fall short of the glory of God" (Romans 3:23).

> "YOUR TALENTS ARE THE CLUE TO WHERE YOU FIT IN THE PROCESS OF EVANGELISM."
>
> —Joseph C. Aldrich

By being obedient, we are allowing God to be what He is best at—*being God.* All we need to do is what He asks us to do; *it is His job to be the Savior of the world.* In fact, we can't save anyone anyway because it is the Holy Spirit who convicts people (John 16:8) of their sins, and without conviction, they will never turn to Christ.

We don't even have to say all the right things, do all the right things, or run ourselves to death trying to "witness" to every person within a 100-mile radius—*and that is very good news!*

God is the only One capable of saving, loving, and caring for everyone on the planet, so we ought to step back, breathe a sigh of relief, and let Him do His job. *That will enable us to do ours.*

People who think they have to be perfect are putting themselves—and everyone around them—under unnecessary and very damaging pressure.

I once heard of a "perfect" Christian girl who led another girl to Christ. The other girl never quite measured up to the "perfect girl" and committed suicide. I'm sure there were additional reasons for this tragic incident, but the "perfect girl" should have at least explained that God's love is not contingent upon our goodness. Rather, He loves us because we are His creation and demonstrated His unconditional love for us by allowing His Son to die for us "while we were still sinners" (Romans 5:8).

God simply loves us for who we are—*no action to prove perfection is required.*

THE SOURCE OF REALITY—A RELATIONSHIP

When I was a young boy, I saw a gasoline-powered airplane in a model shop and decided that I would buy it with my hard-earned money, but my father wouldn't let me. Instead, he bought one himself and let me use it as the template from which to make my own. I did, and learned more about planes and about myself than I could have ever imagined.

> GOD'S LOVE FOR US IS NOT AFFECTED IN THE SLIGHTEST BY WHAT WE SAY OR DO. **THAT IS INCREDIBLE!**

My "new and improved" planes won several awards in local competitions, but I was the real winner—my self-esteem and creativity were boosted into the stratosphere! *What I also learned was that my father, in his denying me what I wanted, was really loving me and wanting the best for me.* As I understood this, my trust for him increased and our relationship deepened.

God is the same, only increasingly so! The more I see His love for me and the more I understand His intent behind His actions, the more I trust Him. In fact, *how could I not trust Him when He loves me unconditionally and has better things in store for me than I could ever dream?* He is the perfect heavenly Father who loves me as I need to be loved. Naturally, our relationship deepens as a result.

This is the very relationship that you hopefully already have that those around you desperately need. And since you have the answer they want, you can be yourself in giving it!

PRESSURE, GUILT, AND OTHER UNNECESSARY FEELINGS

Instead of relaxing and letting God be God, most Christians feel guilty for not doing something "Christian" for the neighbor next door. But when you stop and consider the motivation for these good deeds, it is often based on guilt, condemnation, pressure, or selfishness.

That is not what telling the Good News of Jesus is all about. Yes, it is a priority that we tell others about Christ, *but it is more important that we first love those we are trying to reach out to!*

Acting out of pressure will do far more damage in the long run than acting out of love, even if we don't have all the answers or knowledge. People want to be loved, not preached at.

> **"THE GREAT COMMISSION IS A GROUP PROJECT— JUST DO YOUR PART."**
>
> —Jim Gilbert, *How a man stands up for Christ*

I once knew a man who was his own worst enemy. The troubles he inflicted upon himself were undermining his life, especially his marriage and family. I showed him love and kindness, acted myself around him, and encouraged him when I could. Finally, at the end of his rope, he called me one day literally begging for help. At that moment his heart was really receptive to the forgiveness and new life found only in Jesus Christ.

Thankfully, he made the right decision that day, and as a result, his relationship with his wife and family has been completely restored. Had I tried earlier to "preach" at him out of guilt or pressure, I would only have turned him away from what he needed most.

The answer, I believe, is found in

1. loving God

2. loving others

3. using the talents and gifts that we each have

When we are ourselves, we are real, which is the point that others can see Christ for who He is in you—and if they receive you, they can receive Him.

MY PERSONAL APPROACH

Long ago I decided that my "I'm inadequate" view of telling others about Christ was wrong, and so I chose to believe otherwise. Now when people ask me how I can prove the reality of Christ, I laugh and say, "Jesus controls my life and is alive in my heart. Daily I see Him at work."

How can you refute that?

Others are not so interested in my faith, so I work on them from a different angle. My first step is to put their names in my prayer journal so that I remember to pray daily for them. Writing down their names crystallizes my thoughts—and that begins action.

Then I pray constantly that the Holy Spirit will soften their hearts. I never "point blank them" like a high-pressure salesman, forcing them to make a decision on the spot. People who try to "make the sale" in evangelism fail to realize that evangelism is a way of life. It lasts 365 days a year, so rushing things may do irreparable damage.

Instead, I study people over a period of time while I form a relationship of trust between us. I want them to see how I live, how I relate with my wife, and how I do what I do, all because I want them to see the reality of Christ in every area of my life. Honestly, if I don't have something they want and need, then they won't even be interested in what I have to tell them.

In the meantime, I often give them a nice study Bible with their name on it or find some other practical material that might help them where they are in life. I may even call a pastor in their town who I think will identify with them in some way, such as having an avid interest in fishing, and have them get together in a relaxed setting.

My process is a lot longer, but I wait for the time when it is right and inoffensive to talk with them about my relationship with Christ. I've even told people, "I am glad to see you finally hit bottom."

I genuinely mean it, and they know it. Then I offer more than my prayers—I mix action with my faith and help them find the answers and assistance they need, whether it's marriage counseling, financial advice, or dealing with substance abuse. Whatever caused them to hit the bottom is the best place for me to start helping them.

When God uses me to bring someone to Christ, I want him or her to stay with Christ forever. *It cannot be an emotional decision.*

I once spoke with a young man for an hour, then sent him to a friend who spoke with him for four more hours! My friend was much better at communicating in the style this young man needed, so I let him do it. That evening I saw the young man again—but this time as a new believer in Christ!

Whatever approach works best for you, rest assured that as you live in obedience to God, He will make plain to you what you are to do each step of the way.

WHAT JOY! WHAT NEXT?

> NEW BELIEVERS NEED HELP, ADVICE, PRAYER, FRIENDS, MAYBE SOME COUNSELING, AND DEFINITELY A LOT OF ENCOURAGEMENT.

If you've traveled overseas without a translator, you know how difficult it can be to understand menus, read road signs, find a doctor, use an ATM machine, mail letters, buy clothes, and talk on the telephone, much less do everything else that you would normally do back home. To be dropped off unprepared in such a country would be extremely difficult and very uncomfortable. Without doubt, most would want the next plane home!

Dropping a new believer in Christ off at the starting gate of life is the same thing! Everything is new, from friendships to thoughts and from desires to questions. He or she needs help, advice, prayer, friends, maybe some counseling, and definitely a lot of encouragement.

Sadly, this is where many would-be successes end in failure. The "coming to know Christ" part of the equation lasts a lifetime and is not a one-time event. If you were the one who helped a person into the kingdom of God, then you need to work to ensure that he or she makes it to the finish line, just as Paul said, "I have finished the race, I have kept the faith" (2 Timothy 4:7).

With my newfound friends in Christ, I often can't be there in person, so in addition to praying for them and communicating with them, I try to help them get involved in a good local church and/or tell other friends who live in the area to contact them.

Be creative, but remember that God neither forces Himself on us nor gives us everything so we have no need for faith in Him. This means that new believers in Christ are responsible for their own walk with God—not you.

And because a relationship with Jesus is personal, it only makes sense that you use your own words. It's natural, as is the legacy you leave behind.

THE JOURNEY OF PRAYER

—YOU'LL NEVER BE THE SAME!

Not long ago, someone asked me, "Of all the things that a Christian normally does, such as attend church, fellowship with other believers, worship, pray, read the Bible, etc., what is most important to you?"

Without hesitating I said, "Communicating with God through prayer."

I say this now, but it wasn't always the case. I really didn't pray in earnest until I became a father at age twenty-one. The fact that I was suddenly responsible for something far more important than any job or position I had ever held was a compelling motivation!

MY JOURNEY OF PRAYER

As prayer began to play a greater role in my life, things began to change. Prayer had always seemed dry, boring, and ineffective, but the more I prayed, the more I discovered about life, about God, and about myself—*and it was far from what I had first imagined!*

"Why do I pray?" I asked myself. Before I tried to answer, I took another step back and asked, "What exactly is prayer?"

I know now that prayer is communicating with God, talking to Him, and Him talking back to me, but at that time I was sim-

> PRAYER IS ALL ABOUT A LONG-TERM RELA-TIONSHIP BETWEEN YOU AND GOD.

ply trying to understand what prayer was all about. Archaic English and repetitious phrases were unnecessary; I did know that, but what was a revelation to me was that having an open line of communication between God and myself meant I had to overcome two very real obstacles in my way: barriers and distractions.

#1—BARRIERS

The primary barrier that keeps me from communicating with God is sin (sin is simply doing what God says not to do). I learned it is impossible to communicate with Him if I have something I have not repented for, not because God doesn't love me and doesn't want to talk with me, but because He is Holy—*and holiness and sin do not mix!*

Nevertheless, people often barrel ahead with their prayers, not realizing that Isaiah 59:2 says, "Your iniquities have separated you from your God; your sins have hidden his face from you, so that he will not hear." God never intended that prayer would be an exercise in futility, but it becomes just that when we refuse to repent of our sins.

Does this mean God cannot hear us if we pray with sin in our lives? No, God is merciful and always hears our cries of desperation, but sins we refuse to repent of end up becoming a formidable barrier that can be removed only by choosing to humble ourselves and repent of our actions. A heart that is receptive to the conviction of the Holy Spirit is the secret to living without barriers.

#2—DISTRACTIONS

Distractions that destroy the lines of communication with God are such basic things as being overly tired, sleeping too long, and interruptions (children, phones, TV, music, etc.).

> WHAT MAKES PRAYER SO POWERFUL IS THE FACT THAT GOD SPEAKS TO US—AND WHAT HE SAYS HAS THE ABILITY TO CHANGE OUR LIVES, OUR FAMILY, OUR TOWN, AND OUR COUNTRY!

For most of us, however, the primary distraction is our own lack of discipline. We may have a burning desire to spend time in prayer, but if we aren't willing to discipline ourselves to do it, we won't pray and the passion will fade away.

I have trained myself to pray every morning for an hour before I get out of bed. That is the best time for me, and I am able to focus on my prayers without pondering the concerns of the day. It also prepares me for the decisions, opportunities, and challenges that are sure to come.

Distractions are not usually sins and neither are they blazingly obvious. They are subtle, minor, and of seemingly little consequence, yet they effectively block the lines of communication between us and God.

FIVE REASONS WHY I PRAY

As I tried to answer my "Why am I praying?" question, I began to see prayer in a new light. Here are five reasons why prayer is so important to me:

#1—I LOVE TO PRAY.

If you stop and think about it, talking with the Creator of the universe is no small matter, and that He would want to communicate on a personal level with me is almost incomprehensible! And the more I pray, the closer we get in our relationship. (This is only natural, since the more I communicate with my wife, the more we know each other.)

Yes, there are times when I have a need, but more than for any other reason, I pray because I love God and love to communicate with Him.

#2—I'M NOT IN CONTROL.

I also pray because I'm not in control. The fact of the matter is that *I am never in complete control.* I can control my attitude, my spending habits, and my medication, but there is no way I can control the weather, the stock market, or the actions of other people.

Several years ago my oldest daughter, Janna, was involved in a car accident. Something fell off the seat and she reached for it, simultaneously turning the steering wheel. She looked up in time to put on the brakes before she crashed into a tree. Though the car was damaged, thankfully she escaped without any serious injury—*but it could have easily been worse!*

My heart sank when I heard she had hit a tree, but the relief I felt when I learned she wasn't hurt was indescribable! My love for her had no real control over her. God is the only One in control, so I pray, not out of fear, but out of faith that He will orchestrate events on my behalf.

#3—I NEED HELP.

I love to help people, but I recognize that without God's assistance, my efforts are far from what they could be. Take my friend Dr. J. Clifton "Clif" Williams for instance. He had Hodgkin's disease and the doctors had given him just months to live, so he had put his estate in order and prepared his family for the inevitable.

When I walked into his hospital room, I politely asked everyone to leave so that I could have a few minutes alone with Clif. When they were gone, I talked about Clif's wife, Jan, and their two children, Eric and Lynn, ages six and eight.

Then I brazenly said, "If you seriously want to live, then you need to change your attitude and start visualizing life as if you were going to live and not die! Begin by having an attitude of positive expectancy for life, such as visualizing your kids at their grammar school, high school, and college graduations. What will you be wearing? Where will you go out to eat afterwards?"

I continued, "Until your children leave home for college, what will you do to impress your Christian values on them? Where will you go for family vacations? What have you and Jan always wanted to do together as a family?" On and on my questions went until he began to truly hear and understand what I was trying to say.

"If you want to see tomorrow," I concluded, "then you need to bring the future into present focus through a positive attitude, visualization, and setting goals."

> THROUGH PRAYER, WE WILL NOT CHANGE GOD IN ANY WAY; **WE PRAY AND WE ARE CHANGED OURSELVES.**

I believe it was through a combination of Clif's faith in God, his wife's fervent prayers, the love from his friends and family, and his ability to envision the future that his health was positively affected. Even though he was sick for a couple of years—lymph glands removed, blood transfusions, and diet changes—he slowly and gradually regained his strength. That was twenty-five years ago!

#4—I WANT THINGS TO CHANGE.

Prayer does indeed change things, but the majority of the change takes place in me. There are times when I start to pray for certain people who have been malicious in their comments or actions toward me, and after a period of time, I am the one who ends up changing (forgiving them, but not excusing them).

I've loaned money to people who then refuse to repay what

they owe. As I pray about the issue, several times I have felt that I ought to forgive the debt. I can tell you that it certainly isn't my initial desire to write off money that I am rightfully owed!

As I pray, God uses what has damaged me to bring freedom, blessing, and peace into my life. It is amazing, but every time I pray and do what He says, I come out better off!

Much of what I've gone through was for one reason: God wanting to perfect me. The same applies to you as well. Praying that a hard circumstance will go away might not be to your benefit. Instead, the answer is to pray for His will to be done— then learn to go with the flow.

#5—I NEED TO DO HIS WILL.

If I pray according to my own desires, I am wasting my breath. Jesus was always praying, "Not my will, but yours be done" (Luke 22:42) because He understood His purpose was to accomplish God's will. I have the same purpose, *as does every Christian*, which means my prayers ought to be for what He has for me to do, not for my own selfish desires.

Several years ago I wanted to set up a program to help the economically disadvantaged youth in my town go to college. As I began to pray, God revealed to me an innovative way to make the vision into a reality. As a result, our family set up the Passport to Success Foundation as the financial vehicle to make this possible.

Our actions inspired other Waco families to start their own programs, including Malcolm and Mary Ruth Duncan (the MAC Grant Foundation), Bernard and Audre Rapoport (the Rapoport Foundation), and Clifton and Betsy Robinson (the Clifton Robinson Foundation). *The combined efforts of these foundations have already helped over a thousand disadvantaged youth in our county go to college!*

Jane and I were recently honored by the Texas lieutenant governor and Texas Senate for the effectiveness of the Passport to Success scholarship program. They described our county as probably the only county in the entire United States where a disadvantaged person who wants to attend college is presented with the passport to do so!

THE REALITY OF PRAYER

It didn't take much time in prayer before I discovered another vital ingredient of prayer: obedience. This is the reality of prayer and the reality of a Christian's walk with God. When He speaks, we are to obey, even if it doesn't make sense.

A friend told me of a young missionary woman who was traveling alone in Bangladesh. As she stepped off a bus, she was approached by a family begging for bus fare back to their hometown. The young lady quickly prayed and felt like God was telling her to give them all she had and keep only a few dollars!

For her to give away all her money was a big step of faith, but she obeyed and the family was overjoyed. When they walked away to buy tickets, the missionary turned to leave. Before she had taken more than twenty steps, a thief wielding a knife demanded her money. With a smile on her face, she almost laughed as she gave him all she had—just a few dollars!

> "UNLESS THE VITAL FORCES OF PRAYER ARE SUPPLIED BY GOD'S WORD, PRAYER, THOUGH EARNEST, EVEN VOCIFEROUS, IN ITS URGENCY, IS, IN REALITY, FLABBY AND VAPID AND VOID."
>
> —E. M. Bounds

Obedience protects, directs, and catapults us to heights we could never have imagined otherwise. How quick we forget that "anyone, then, who knows the good he ought to do and doesn't do it, sins" (James 4:17). Though obedience is really our only option, *it is always to our benefit!*

We can accomplish all that God has for us individually

when we hear (through prayer) what God has to say to us and then do what He commands us to do. With His help, we can even do the impossible, because "with God all things are possible" (Matthew 19:26).

WHAT MAKES PRAYER EFFECTIVE

For prayer to be effective, faith is required. Scripture says "faith comes by hearing, and hearing by the word of God" (Romans 10:17, NKJV). This reality came in stages for me.

One day I read "God is love" (1 John 4:8) and my eyes were opened like never before! If God is love, then it follows that He cannot be mean, cruel, hateful, spiteful, or selfish. It is impossible! Everything He does is then based in what He is—complete and perfect love.

When it clicked in my mind that God's plans for me are good (Jeremiah 29:11), I realized that He actually *wants* to answer my prayers. I was amazed!

Another time John 15:7 also came to life. It says, "If you abide in Me, and My words abide in you, you will ask what you desire, and it shall be done for you." When His Word resides in my heart, what I ask for comes to pass? Incredible! *(And it has been!)*

The number of such faith-building revelations is limitless, but the crux of the matter is this: without faith, prayer accomplishes virtually nothing . . . but with faith, anything is possible!

TRACKING ANSWERS IN A JOURNAL

Many years ago I began to list in my prayer journal the names of people who needed prayer. This, and a brief note beside their name, helped me not to forget anyone and to be more focused in my prayers. When a prayer was answered, I put the date beside it. It wasn't long before my journal had an extensive track record of answered prayers.

Rereading those answered prayers refreshes me and fills me with faith to keep praying, keep believing, and keep expecting God to move on my behalf.

> "GOD DOES NOTHING BUT IN ANSWER TO PRAYER."
>
> —John Wesley

It is natural for faith to increase every time God answers a prayer, but it is also natural for faith to decrease when we forget the answers to prayer that we have received. For me, I can't forget what God has done because I see it in black and white.

In my journal are many different lists, each marked with a distinct title and colored tab. Some of the topics include: my personal and family concerns, the ministries that are close to my heart, friends and acquaintances, health concerns of various people, and the names of people who have hurt me.

Under the title of each section I write specific affirmations. For example, under my "Charities and Ministries" title I have several affirmations, including the following:

My Affirmation:

* I believe God has given me the gift of stewardship,
    I earn to give,
    I live to share,
    I multiply my personal ministry by giving in Jesus' name!

* *"God loves a cheerful giver!"*
    —2 Corinthians 9:7, NEB

* *"Give and it will be given unto you—good measure pressed down—shaken together—for with the measure you use it will be measured to you."*
    —Luke 6:38

* *"But whoever has this world's goods, and sees his brother in need, and shuts up his heart from him, how does the love of God abide in him? My little children, let us not love in word or tongue, but in deed and*

in truth."

—1 John 3:17–18 NKJV

Under the affirmations I write the names and the needs of the people and ministries I am praying for. As I begin to pray for these people, a whole new dimension of prayer opens up—intercession.

Intercession is powerful! I have seen rebellious children change, marriages restored, dismal financial situations improve, and people's hard hearts melt with compassion, all as a result of my prayers, and who knows how many other people's prayers. Being steadfast, tenacious, and consistent in prayer will move mountains, whether for ourselves or for other people. Beside these individuals' names I write Scriptures I pray over them, answers to prayer, new prayers, ideas, comments, and words I feel God is giving me.

As I go through my journal, there are times when I only pray for other people. Some days I spend the entire time thanking God for His goodness to me. Other days I pray about what concerns me, such as asking God for wisdom, health, guidance, and protection from the Enemy's temptations.

Utilizing a prayer journal to its full potential does take discipline, just as prayer does, but the benefits will always outweigh the efforts!

> "THE GREATEST LEGACY WE EVER COULD LEAVE OUR CHILDREN AND THEIR CHILDREN IS THEIR SEEING AND KNOWING THE IMPORTANCE AND POWER OF FAMILY PRAYER."
> —Evelyn Christenson

PRAYER REQUIRES ACTION

In addition to praying, I help in a practical manner as well. While praying, I often feel I need to do something for that person, which has included mailing books, writing letters, making phone calls, giving speeches, postponing meetings, canceling trips, and more. The results have been astounding!

One family I met appeared on the surface to have a perfect life. They were a great couple who had good jobs and fabulous children, but during several conversations with them, I began to sense that all was not well.

They were in financial straits and were in some denial about personal problems, which led me to believe that their relationship was strained. It was my view that the reason for their dilemma was the fact that neither the parents nor the children had a personal relationship with Christ.

We talked numerous times, I had an accountant help them with their finances, and I gave them several books. Many months later, Jane and I were very pleased when the father called to tell us that the entire family had accepted Christ! As this family moves forward in their Christian journey, it is exciting to watch as every previous problem that was a part of their life is being resolved.

HE WANTS TO ANSWER OUR PRAYERS

We must believe that God hears, that He cares, and that He acts on our behalf. That is faith.

Jesus said, "Ask and it will be given to you; seek and you will find; knock and the door will be opened to you" (Matthew 7:7). It takes effort to ask, seek, and knock until an answer comes.

Instead of an immediate answer, we often experience delay. Delay, however, works to test the strength of our faith, and faith in turn gathers strength by waiting and praying. *Faith has nothing to do with time and everything to do with trusting God.*

I have had prayers answered that took many years to be answered. But had I never prayed, I don't believe the answer would have come! In fact, some of my most meaningful and encouraging answers to prayer came after several years of praying.

Does this mean that God answers every prayer I have ever

prayed? Yes, I believe He does answer all my prayers, though not necessarily in the way I might want.

I find great comfort in the fact that God knows "how to give good gifts" much better than I do and that "everyone who asks receives; he who seeks finds; and to him who knocks, the door will be opened" (Matthew 7:11, 8). The fact is, He desires to answer our prayers—we just need to be willing to do our part through diligent prayer, faith, and action.

> "THE TIME TO LEARN HOW TO PRAY IS NOW, NOT WHEN A CRISIS ARISES."
>
> —George A. Brantley, author and pastor

Prayer allows God's power to be revealed and His plans to come to pass. Through prayer, I have experienced God's power, wisdom, favor, and creativity in my life to a degree that I could never have imagined!

As a result of prayer, my world has changed and I know I'll never be the same . . . *and neither will you!*

PART TWO

ATTITUDES FOR LIVING THE CHRISTIAN LIFE

ATTITUDE IS EVERYTHING!

—DISCOVERING THE KEYS FOR **ALL** SUCCESS

Is attitude really everything? Obviously, from a Christian point of view, attitude is not everything—Christ is every thing. So, where did I get the phrase "Attitude is everything"?

Early in my insurance career I recruited some incredibly gifted and talented people, but, as I used to say, "He looks good in uniform, but he can't bat." The problem was that these people had developed or been programmed with a negative mental attitude and therefore could not produce.

Repetitively dealing with people who needed a complete attitude overhaul showed me the importance of attitude and was the underlying inspiration behind my first company, Success Motivation Institute. I've been called the "founder of the personal development industry" as a result of the age and success of SMI—*and it all started with attitude!*

> **"WE CAN ALTER OUR LIVES BY ALTERING OUR ATTITUDES OF MIND."**
>
> —William James

In the twenty-four personal development programs I've written in almost fifty years, I've often stated that "attitude is a habit of thought—if you want to change your attitude, you must change the way you think."

Changing the way you think is not a new concept. Scripture states very clearly, "Your attitude should be the same as that of Christ Jesus" (Philippians 2:5) and "whatever is true . . . noble . . . right . . . pure . . . lovely . . . admirable—if anything is excellent or praiseworthy—think about such things" (Philippians 4:8).

Olympic athletes, coaches, successful people, and achievers in any area all love the phrase, "Attitude is everything." Why is that? I believe it is because they not only understand it, but they *live it* as well.

To celebrate my seventieth year, I climbed Mount Elbert, the tallest of Colorado's fourteen highest peaks and the second tallest mountain in the continental U.S. This might not seem like an impressive feat, but just three weeks before I had walked out of a respiratory hospital (the National Jewish Center in Denver, Colorado) where I had been admitted with a severe asthma attack. What's more, there is less oxygen after 12,000 feet, and Mount Elbert has an elevation of 14,431 feet! Only a few people know that I crawled the last 500 feet on my hands and knees. Breathing was difficult and movement was slow, but at that precise moment, *attitude was everything!*

> LIFE IS 10 PERCENT WHAT HAPPENS TO ME AND 90 PERCENT HOW I REACT TO IT.

ATTITUDE IS BASIC TO SURVIVAL

Who you are is *not* determined by how you look, where you live, or who your parents were. *Who you are is a function of specific choices that you have made.* You are where you are and what you are because of the dominating thoughts in your mind.

After all, as a man "thinks in his heart, so is he" (Proverbs 23:7 NKJV).

Several years ago, a plastic surgeon friend of mine, Dr. Robert Gardere, made a study of the people on whom he had performed cosmetic surgery. Each of the people had come to him asking for some change because they were unhappy with how they looked. As a surgeon, he gave them new noses, took away their wrinkles, or made some other significant changes in their appearance. But Dr. Gardere discovered something quite unexpected: Most of the people thought the surgery had been a failure because they were still dissatisfied with themselves.

> YOU ARE WHERE YOU ARE AND WHAT YOU ARE BECAUSE OF THE DOMINATING THOUGHTS IN YOUR MIND.

The conclusion is obvious: *We are what we think we are—not what we appear to be on the outside.*

ATTITUDE IS BONE DEEP

I saw a movie once about a convicted thief who was offered a chance for a new life. After a complete makeover to change his appearance and altered fingerprints, there was nothing left to tie him to his old self. He became extremely successful . . . for a while.

He reverted to a life of crime and was shot by a policeman. As he lay dying, he said, "The doctors didn't know, did they?" The doctors had changed him on the outside, but they had done nothing to change him on the inside *where all the significant and lasting change begins.*

I learned this as a young man. I knew in my heart that I would not pick fruit for the rest of my life; yet I still did it to make money. On the inside I was different from most of the other young people I worked with. Over time, the outside lined up with what my inside believed and I never returned to manual labor again. That is because changes on the outside will inevitably match what the heart and mind have already decided to do or be.

My favorite poem about attitude is one by Japan's Tomihiro Hoshino, an author and painter who is also quadriplegic due to a gymnastic accident. In *Road of the Tinkling Bell*, he wrote,

> *Wind is invisible*
> *Yet*
> *blowing through the trees*
> *it becomes a green wind*
> *And*
> *breathing on the flowers*
> *it becomes a flower wind*
> *Now*
> *the wind caresses my face*
> *Well then, I wonder,*
> *what kind of wind*
> *will it become*
> *now?*

Each of us has an overall pattern of thinking that is generally either positive or negative. The pattern you choose has four profound effects on your life:

#1—YOUR BASIC ATTITUDE AFFECTS YOUR BELIEF IN YOUR POTENTIAL FOR SUCCESS.

A negative attitude causes you to doubt your ability to achieve, while belief in your potential makes you willing to take the necessary action for success.

#2—YOUR ATTITUDE DETERMINES WHAT YOU THINK ABOUT FACING A CHALLENGE.

A positive attitude lets you see a challenge as an opportunity rather than a threat.

#3—YOUR ATTITUDE DETERMINES YOUR CONFIDENCE.

People with negative attitudes have so often thought, "I can't" or "I doubt," that belief in their individual potential is nonexistent. Each time you act from a positive attitude, your self-confidence is enhanced, your ability to achieve is proven, and you know you can succeed.

#4—YOUR ATTITUDE AFFECTS HOW YOU SEE OPPORTUNITY.

People who have a negative attitude have buried the ability to see opportunity. A positive attitude, by contrast, opens your eyes to so many opportunities that your challenge becomes which opportunity to choose.

HOW TO FORM ATTITUDES

The benefits of a positive attitude are available when you understand how an attitude is formed. You

| ATTITUDE IS A HABIT OF THOUGHT. |

then have the option to control the process and form the attitude you want.

There are three basic steps to forming an attitude:

First—the first step in attitude formation is input. Everything since birth is used by our subconscious mind as input from which attitudes are formed.

When we are older and realize we need to change our attitudes, we obviously can't start over at birth. What we can do, however, is change the input. This has a way of positively affecting our mind and our entire body, as Scripture clearly states, "Be transformed by the renewing of your mind" (Romans 12:2).

Second—the second step in the formation of attitudes is personal processing of inputs. As you have heard what other people said to you and observed what they did in their own lives, you processed that information and chose your attitudes. As you acted on your chosen belief, it gradually became established as a habit of thought—an attitude.

My chosen belief is that I can do anything. I wake up each day without the mental recognition of the possibility of defeat. This is my attitude and it affects everything I do, say, or think.

> "FAME IS A VAPOR; POPULARITY AN ACCIDENT; RICHES TAKE WINGS; ONLY ONE THING ENDURES—CHARACTER."
>
> —Horace Greeley

Third—the third and final element in the development of attitude is reinforcement. When you make a tentative choice of an attitude, it eventually becomes firmly entrenched by reinforcement as you follow it day after day.

These three—input, processing of input, and reinforcement—form a 1-2-3 series that naturally and automatically work together. There is nothing mystical about it. It simply happens.

Now suppose you become aware that some specific attitude is holding you back from the success and achievement you are capable of attaining. Can you change that attitude? Yes, you can!

Changing a habit of action or thought is not simple or necessarily quick, but it is certainly possible. *You must first make a conscious choice to change!* Breaking the old cycle of habit formation is the key to changing your attitudes.

The following principle hits the nail right on the head:

- ◆ Sow a thought, reap an action,
- ◆ Sow an action, reap a habit,
- ◆ Sow a habit, reap character,
- ◆ Sow character, reap a destiny.

THREE BIG CHANGES: THOUGHT, SPEECH, AND BEHAVIOR

As you work to change your attitude, remember that attitudes operate on three planes: thought, speech, and behavior.

What you fill your mind with is eventually translated into the words you speak, and then your words are put into action. If you are not pleased with your results, you can intervene in the process of attitude formation at any one of the three points of thought, words, or behavior.

#1—WORKING ON YOUR THOUGHTS

You must be aware of what goes on in your head before you can change it. Whenever you catch yourself thinking, "I can't" or "I'm afraid" or "That's too risky," stop and tell yourself, "Look again. I'll give this opportunity a chance. I can do it!"

Or make up your own success message, such as, "I know I can do this" or "The righteous will never be uprooted, but the wicked will not remain in the land" (Proverbs 10:30). The important thing to do is to *break the automatic negative thought pattern.*

> "IMMENSE POWER IS ACQUIRED BY ASSURING YOURSELF IN YOUR SECRET REVERIES THAT YOU WERE BORN TO CONTROL AFFAIRS."
> —Andrew Carnegie

I once worked with a group of professional salespeople for six months before I saw a noticeable change in their thought patterns. When their thinking finally changed, their sales increased.

#2—CHANGING YOUR SPEECH PATTERNS

Listen to yourself as you talk. How often do you use negative words? How often do you express doubt, lack of confidence in your ability, or fear?

Write out some positive words to use the next time the chance arises. Be sure these words express the kind of success attitude you want to adopt. Practice long enough that you will remember the positive words when you need them.

#3—MODIFYING BEHAVIOR

Everyone reacts differently to the same stresses. A friend of mine was given a challenging project at work and instead of starting it, he went and slouched in front of the TV. When he realized what he was doing, he made the conscious effort to get started on the project, which needed to be done sooner or later anyway.

Intervening at the point of behavior is often the easiest point at which you can begin to make a change. Where you intervene is up to you, for your personality is unique and your abilities are different.

HOW TO INTERVENE

One of the most effective ways to intervene is to make use of the Power Mind Principle to change your attitude, which involves using a highly controlled practice of visualization, according to a specific plan, designed to accomplish a definite purpose.

Here is how it works:

A. Begin by spending some time in quiet relaxation. Put aside worries, fears, and anxieties for the moment. Consider Proverbs 16:3, which says, "Commit to the LORD whatever you do, and your plans will succeed."

B. Read some passage you have found or one that you have written for yourself that describes the attitude or belief *you want to adopt* as your own.

C. Actively visualize yourself acting, speaking, or feeling in accordance with that attitude or belief.

D. And finally, through visualization, you actually experience the behavior. You are eliminating old negative conditioning and providing new positive change.

Attitudes, because they are habits of thought, do not happen overnight. You will not change them with one attempt, *so be patient and give yourself time to absorb enough new, positive input to make the desired change.*

Plan positive reinforcement to reward yourself when you succeed. Positive affirmations serve this purpose well; here are a few:

- That feels great! I can permanently change my thoughts, words, or behavior about this.

- I can see progress already. I am willing to persist to see greater change!

- My plan is working—I will succeed!

Measure your progress by comparing where you are now to where you were when you started. This encourages you to continue your efforts to grow by proving that growth is possible. Then look ahead to where you would like to be as a means of inspiration to keep growing.

> "WE ARE WHAT WE REPEATEDLY DO; EXCELLENCE, THEN, IS NOT AN ACT, BUT A HABIT."
> —Aristotle

It is at this point that I turn my attention toward being thankful to God for the change that has taken place in my life. Being thankful is an important part of the reinforcement process.

BENEFITS OF A POSITIVE ATTITUDE

Changing your attitude takes time and effort, but it is well worth whatever it costs you. The benefits of a positive attitude are outstanding:

1. increased enthusiasm

2. freedom from the limitations of fear

3. increased creativity

4. enjoyment in taking the initiative

5. exciting joy when using more of your God-given potential

6. boundless opportunities

7. abundance of positive friends and colleagues

8. increased efficiency in utilizing your time and energy

Does having a positive attitude mean that you will never make a mistake? No, not at all, but it is important to learn that there is more profit in making a few mistakes than in avoiding them altogether. Those who have too great a fear of making mistakes will take no risks, and though they won't make any mistakes, neither will they learn or grow. Meet challenges head on, and you will gain—even from your losses.

Depending on your attitude, every obstacle, challenge, and problem has the potential to be the best thing that ever happened to you. The attitudes you choose are the keys to unlimited success.

That is precisely why they say, "Attitude is everything!"

LIVING LIFE WITH AN ATTITUDE OF GRATITUDE

—BECAUSE LIFE IS WHAT YOU MAKE OF IT

Several years ago I heard of two brothers who were counseled by a psychologist at their mother's request. She was concerned about the boys' extreme attitudes—one was excessively positive, the other excessively negative.

The psychologist isolated each boy in a different room for twelve hours. In the negative boy's room were hundreds of toys and every carnival ride imaginable. The overly positive boy's room was prepared like a horse stall in a barn and very dark.

After the twelve hours were up, the door to the first room was opened to reveal the negative boy crying by the door. When asked why he wasn't playing with the toys, he complained through his tears, "I knew that if I played with something I would probably get hurt."

Next, the doctor went to the room that resembled a dark horse

> **"LEARNING TO BE THANKFUL COVERS IT ALL."**
>
> —Charlie "Tremendous" Jones

stall. When he opened the door, he found the positive boy digging through the hay, laughing and screaming with delight. When the doctor got him quieted down, the boy exclaimed, "I know there is a pony in here somewhere, and I'm going to find him!"

The boys' attitudes were amazingly consistent, regardless of the circumstances. *So it is with us.*

LIFE IS WHAT YOU MAKE OF IT

From birth to the grave we are insulted, left out, taken advantage of, and discounted—and that's only from people, let alone the other negative things that might happen in life! The fact is that much of what life gives you is not all that great.

But when you view your world through the eyes of positive expectancy, like the boy looking for the pony, you are training yourself to focus on the good in life. It isn't that you ignore the bad things or pretend that everything is perfect—to do so is to live in a dream world. *Life is real, which means you will encounter both good and bad.*

Having a positive attitude is admittedly a good thing, but there is one more ingredient that will propel your positive view of life to the next level: gratefulness.

GRATEFUL FOR TEMPORARY SETBACKS

> "KEEP YOUR FACE TO THE SUNSHINE AND YOU CANNOT SEE A SHADOW."
>
> —Helen Keller

We have all had our fair share of setbacks and disappointments. Of the 100 companies I've started since the age of nineteen, 65 percent have not survived. They could in an ordinary sense be called "failures," but in my mind and with my positive attitude, I've never considered that I've ever failed at anything.

These supposed failures were only temporary setbacks. I

never took it personally or thought of myself as a lesser person. On the contrary, I was grateful for each setback. *I know that in every adversity there is a seed of equivalent or greater benefit if I believe it, look for it, and work for it.* When you have that belief and follow through, you will always find the benefit you are looking for.

These "failures" enabled me to learn a practical lesson by studying why the concept, business, or idea did not work. What's more, I was tougher mentally and smarter going into the next situation. *How could I not be grateful?*

When you place the bad beside the good, the negative beside the positive, you gain a whole new perspective about life, one that almost delights in the bad because you are so accustomed to the greater good that is coming next!

Here are just a few examples:

THE NEGATIVE	THE POSITIVE
My dad wouldn't let me buy a model airplane at the hobby shop.	He showed me how to design and build my own from raw materials and I won awards for it!
My dad wouldn't let me buy my first bicycle.	I learned how to restore old bicycles—and made money doing it!
We didn't have a television until I was sixteen.	I was an inventor, reader, mechanic, builder, workman, field manager, and more.
My father was a tough disciplinarian.	I learned how to be disciplined.
My first job in the insurance industry was starting at the very bottom.	I had the privilege of starting as an apprentice and learning it from the bottom up.
I had a lot of competition from others at work.	I worked harder and performed better because of the competition.
A plane I was flying lost all hydraulic control and we crashed in a corn field.	I walked away with only a gash to my elbow.
A truck forced me and my bicycle off the road.	I'm grateful I escaped with only lacerations to my hand.
I've encountered prejudice and racism.	Now I'm very sensitive to those around me.

The bad/negative times were a perfect breeding ground for success and breakthrough. Instead of letting the hard times get me down, I've learned to keep going and to look for the good that I know is hidden in there somewhere. Usually it isn't until later that I see the benefit for the negative I just experienced.

By training myself to believe that good will always be the result, it's simply hard not to be grateful!

> "LIFE IS RICH IN REWARDS TO A PERSON WHO HAS LEARNED TO BE THANKFUL IN ANY AND EVERY CIRCUMSTANCE."
>
> —Bill Bunting

ONE BY ONE

The old classic hymn that said, "Count your blessings, name them one by one. Count your blessings, see what God hath done . . ." may sound outdated, but the principle is not. When we name or write down our blessings, it burns into our subconscious the fact that we have much to be grateful for.

A friend of mine has a young son who went through a severe bout with cancer. Thankfully the cancer is completely gone, but while they were fighting the sickness in the hospital, the family learned to be grateful for every day, one day at a time.

When you look at a bright light and then close your eyes, what do you see? You see that same light even with your eyes closed. Keep your eyes closed and that light will slowly fade away. It is the same with gratitude. By writing down what you are grateful for, you are impressing it over and over into your mind, making it all the more difficult for you to forget.

I know a couple who every month write down in a special notebook all the things they are grateful for. At the end of the next month they read the previous month's list before they make a new list. They are training themselves—and their children—to view life through eyes of gratefulness.

What's more, writing something down dramatically increases your chances of remembering it. I see it like this: If your favorite team is playing a rival team for the championship, you are interested in one primary detail—the score at the end of the game. Admittedly, it would be absurd to play without keeping score, but the fact of the matter is that we often go through life without keeping score. *We don't write things down, and as a result, we don't remember long-term who won.*

> IT IS OUR NATURE TO FORGET. THAT IS, HOWEVER, NO EXCUSE FOR FORGETTING.

Write it down, memorize it, reread it, or make it into a song; do whatever you have to do to be grateful! The Bible records multiple instances where the Israelites "forgot what He had done" (i.e., Psalm 78:11) and reverted back to the former attitudes and actions that got them in trouble in the first place. They saw the very miracles that we make movies about—yet they forgot!

To tell you the honest truth, it is our nature to forget. That is, however, no excuse for forgetting.

BEING GRATEFUL REQUIRES POSITIVE RECALL

One of the few times it is healthy to look back is when you are being grateful. Usually, looking back will do nothing but slow you down or even trip you up. Here are six of the many things I have written down over the years that I'm grateful for, though some are more personal than others, each one is special to me:

#1—FAMILY

My parents—I will forever be grateful to my parents for what they taught me, implanted into my heart and mind, and "denied" me.

Together they taught me to live, to dream, and to be disciplined enough to get where I wanted to go. They showed me by example that if I could control my heart and mind, I could control my actions and therefore my future. By denying me the easy way out, they were forcing me to learn how to free myself.

If it weren't for them and their unique ways of teaching, showing, and living, I would be a completely different person.

My wife—Jane is my best friend. She knows me, the inner me, and she loves me all the more. I often say that when I grow up I want to be like her, and I mean it! She is the perfect balance between work and family, intensity and lightness. Her countenance is always the same: joy, peace, and happiness. Perhaps some day when I grow up . . . .

My children—My five children make me the proudest father in the world. And their children, my grandchildren, are icing on the cake! God has blessed me through my children in so many ways. How each of them has stood up for what is right in his or her own way has been a delight to see. They have all made the most important decision of all—accepting Jesus into their hearts—and they are all growing and maturing in their areas of influence. Sometimes I think, "I don't deserve to have such a blessed family," but I certainly won't complain about it!

#2—FRIENDS

I've been the luckiest person in the world. I have had countless friends over the years who have been there when I needed them most. One friend gave me a handful of cash when I needed it desperately—and we both

> **TO YOUR HEALTH!**
>
> IN ONE STUDY, PEOPLE WHO WERE GRATEFUL ON A DAILY BASIS HAD "HIGHER REPORTED LEVELS OF ALERTNESS, ENTHUSIASM, DETERMINATION, ATTENTIVENESS AND ENERGY."
>
> —Robert A. Emmons, professor of psychology at the University of California, Davis

started to cry. Another friend listened to me vent my frustrations about life and my career, only to tell me that he believed in me and that I ought to pursue my dreams.

Several friends challenged me to give more to worthy causes. Now as I give I think, "This isn't fair, I'm having too much fun!" I'm thankful they pushed me in the right direction. Other friends have told me the honest truth about something I was doing, and I accepted their advice and changed. Why not? It was to my benefit!

All told, my friends have made a tremendous impact in my life—and I'm so grateful for them.

#3—PROTECTION AND FAVOR

I've walked away from many potentially deadly accidents, including three plane crashes. God has protected me so many times that I can't help but think that He has a special purpose for me.

He has also granted me extreme favor with people. I've walked into businesses and been greeted with, "I don't know what you are selling, but I'm going to buy some." Other times I've been in the right place at the right time and overheard a business deal that turned out to be highly lucrative for me. I could have been ten seconds late or early and missed it, but instead I was right there and benefited from it.

It's never luck, but rather a blessing from God.

#4—HARD TIMES AND GOOD CHARACTER

Hard times do indeed bring good character. I've faced extreme pressure as a salesman that caused me to fly higher, fight stronger, and stay longer. In the end I won by a margin that my competitors couldn't touch!

Pressure on carbon produces a diamond over time, and I've come to accept pressure as a good thing—*because I know the value of what is being refined in me.*

> **"INGRATITUDE IS THE ESSENCE OF VILENESS."**
> —Immanuel Kant
> (1724–1804)

The Russian proverb that states, "The same hammer that shatters the glass forges the steel" is true. If we have a positive attitude, adversities and difficulties can only make us stronger and more confident.

Hard times may bring good character, but "hard times" are *not* synonymous with "bad days." The truth is, positive people don't have bad days! I wouldn't know a bad day if I were in the middle of one. How can I have a bad day when I know I'm going to win, when Christ is in my heart, and when I look forward to what I will gain? Failure is really only a temporary setback that turns a hard time into an opportunity and a "bad day" into a good day.

#5—ANSWERED PRAYERS

Countless times I have prayed for the impossible concerning people, relationships, jobs, etc., and then found that God has taken over and done more than I could have asked or imagined. The Bible does say that the "prayer of the righteous man is powerful and effective" (James 5:16) and I believe it with all my heart. I am so grateful that God hears my prayers.

Not long ago the mother of a young man called to say that her son had recently accepted Christ while traveling in a foreign country. Five years earlier I had spoken with him at his mother's request and found he was not interested in anything I said. I placed him on my prayer list and began to pray for him. Though it took some time, the mother's call that day was an extremely encouraging answer to prayer.

It is interesting to note that we are commanded in Scripture to "continue earnestly in prayer, being vigilant in it with thanksgiving" (Colossians 4:2 NKJV). Thanksgiving and prayer go hand in hand.

#6—FORGIVENESS, LOVE, AND MERCY

Lastly, and most important, I am grateful for what God has done for me. Words cannot express my appreciation for Him sending His Son to die on the cross for me. And not only did He make a way for me to receive forgiveness of my sins and to have my relationship with God be restored, but He planted people in my life who told me about Christ's offer.

What Jesus did for me is incredible, but the fact that He told me about it through other people shows me just how much He cares for me. Advances in technology are enabling us to discover galaxies where we first thought only a few stars were located. In the vastness of it all, I have been singled out by the Creator!

That is truly amazing!

- - - - - - -

There are obviously many, many more things to be grateful for, but once you start keeping track, you'll discover there is no place to stop. Living with an attitude of gratitude is without a doubt the best way to live life.

MIRRORING YOUR POSITIVE SELF-IMAGE

—HOW YOU SEE YOURSELF IS HOW OTHERS SEE YOU

One absolutely essential ingredient for success in any endeavor is that of a positive self-image. That is because the world operates on the basis of the law of attraction: *What you are and what you think will attract corresponding conditions.*

If you have a negative self-image, you attract negative results. If your self-image is positive, you attract positive results. This may appear simplistic, *but it is absolutely true!*

WHAT IS YOUR SELF-IMAGE?

Your self-image is your mental picture of yourself and is made up of these six important ingredients:

1. what you believe about your talents and abilities

2. what you believe about your worth as a person

3. how you expect others to accept you

4. what you believe you can become

5. what you expect your world to be like

6. what you believe about how you came into existence

The mental picture you have of yourself determines the measure of confidence you bring to the challenge of using your potential and working toward the achievement of your goals.

> WHAT PEOPLE BUY OF YOU IS THE IMAGE YOU HAVE OF YOURSELF . . . THAT YOU CONVEY TO THEIR SUBCONSCIOUS MIND BY YOUR PRESENCE, PERSONA, CHARISMA, AND WORD CHOICE.

Psychologists estimate that we use considerably less than a third of our actual potential. This means that by increasing your potential just slightly, you can make a sizable improvement in your effectiveness.

If, for example, you are now using 30 percent of your potential, you could choose to use an additional 3 percent—a total of 33 percent of your potential. This additional 3 percent is equal to 10 percent of what you were previously using. So, with relatively little effort, you can be 10 percent more effective than you are now.

Similarly, a small increase in your self-image will reap big dividends. As you seek to improve your self-image, it is important to recognize that most of us have three separate self-images, which include:

A. the "me" I really am (this is your true potential)

B. the "me" I think I am (how realistic this is depends upon how well you know yourself)

C. the "me" I want to become (this image can expand when you discover more of your true potential)

For me, I want to be the perfect husband ("C"—who I want to become) and sometimes I think I do a pretty good job ("B"—who I think I am), but to get the most accurate reading ("A"—who I really am), you would have to ask my wife.

The closer these three images are the better. People who have a distorted picture of their real inner being never discover how great they could be; their potential is a sleeping giant.

Self-image is built day by day from experiences, from what other people say and do, and from how you respond to all of these occurrences. If you respond with the same emotion, feeling, or action every time you meet similar circumstances, that response becomes a habit and your subconscious mind then tells you that this is the kind of person you are. *You have just built a part of your self-image.*

> WHAT YOU DO IS IMPORTANT, BUT WHAT YOU DO IS MERELY A RESULT OF WHO YOU ARE.

Your self-image is therefore the result of choices you make. If you made some unwise choices when you were inexperienced, frightened, immature, or pressured, it is possible to change the self-image that resulted from those choices.

Despite what certain fields of thought have been—that we have no real control over our choices or that our choices are simply the result of past conditioning—*we do indeed have control over our choices!* Knowing that I can control my future motivates me, excites me, and gives me hope for a better tomorrow, while believing otherwise results in the opposite.

The truth is, we can build a new self-image (one that is a more accurate picture of our real, God-given potential) the same way we built our present self-image—*by exercising our power of choice.*

CAN I REALLY CHANGE MY SELF-IMAGE?

Your mind works like a computer. It stores all the information you give it and uses this information to formulate your thoughts, which means:

A. Your present (who you are and where you are today) is a result of your past choices.

B. Your future will be the result of what you are thinking about now.

Your self-image is the direct result of all you have given your subconscious mind as a database. If your self-image is negative, it is because you have chosen negative responses to life. If it is positive, it is because you chose to think and act positively.

In other words, you are responsible for your own self-image.

SEVEN BARRIERS TO A POSITIVE SELF-IMAGE

Regardless of your background, what you are willing to become is the only reality that counts. And what you are willing to become depends greatly upon what you believe and what you are willing to do about your self-image.

Some people, however, allow artificial barriers to limit their potential for success. Why do they do this? I believe it is because they have let one or more of the following seven attitudes hinder them from using more of their potential:

1. *"I'm comfortable."*—Staying in the comfort zone and living at the present level of success is easier and less stressful than exerting effort to make needed changes.

2. *"I'm afraid of failure."*—Fear of making a mistake or risking possible failure discourages trying anything new or different.

3. *"Disapproval hurts."*—The desire to avoid disapproval, either by themselves or by others, limits many to behavior that is calculated to please.

4. *"I don't want to rock the boat."*—Anxiety about changing the

status quo convinces some that change is negative and not worth the risk.

5. *"I don't have what it takes."*—A poverty mentality, coupled with a false sense of inferiority, causes some people to believe they do not deserve the rewards of using their full potential.

6. *"Success might not be good for me."*—An illogical fear of success prevents many from breaking the success barrier. They feel unworthy or they fear they will not know how to handle success, so they subconsciously avoid it.

7. *"God doesn't want me to succeed."*—This unfounded belief of God sends many great dreams into a tailspin. Scripture says, "I pray that you may prosper *in all things* and be in health, just as your soul prospers" (3 John 1:2 NKJV, emphasis mine).

Success will mean something different to everyone because we all view life through our own uniquely tinted pair of glasses. The success you seek can become reality when you exchange limiting beliefs for a more positive self-image.

> YOUR SELF-IMAGE IS BUILT LITTLE BY LITTLE, DAY BY DAY, FROM YOUR EXPERIENCES, FROM WHAT OTHER PEOPLE SAY AND DO, AND FROM HOW YOU RESPOND TO ALL OF THESE OCCURRENCES.

HOW TO STRENGTHEN YOUR POSITIVE SELF-IMAGE

Purposefully choosing to strengthen your self-image is an amazing possibility and the rewards and benefits will last for a lifetime, so keep pressing in and pressing on—then you can press *through* anything! Along the way, don't be discouraged if it takes effort and time. Nothing worth getting in life is ever free, but the payoff at the end will be worth every ounce of effort.

The following four-step plan will help strengthen your positive self-image:

1. *Learn the power of dreams.* A goal begins as a dream. Unless you can imagine something new, you have nowhere to go except where you have been. Look up! Discover a dream that is so important you are willing to commit your life to it. Dreams give you the ability to see the possible, visualize it as the probable, and transform it into reality. Your dream will bring focus like never before.

2. *Cultivate a burning desire to reach your dreams.* Desire spells the difference between mere daydreams and goals. Desire kindles motivation, builds enthusiasm, sparks creativity, and triggers action. Desire can be cultivated by keeping your purpose and goals before you daily. Review the benefits of achieving them and desire will burn within you.

3. *Exercise your freedom of choice.* Act on your freedom to choose—or lose it. If you hesitate, others will choose for you and tell you what to do, directing you toward *their* goals, not yours. Use your freedom of choice to design a stronger, more positive self-image for yourself. If you are fearful, choose courage. If you are timid, choose to love people. If you frequently procrastinate, choose to take action now. If you have always waited for others to lead, choose to act on your own initiative now.

4. *Learn who you are and what your Creator says you can do.* Scripture says, "If anyone is in Christ, he is a new creation; the old has gone, the new has come!" (2 Corinthians 5:17) and "I can do everything through him who gives me strength" (Philippians 4:13). Knowing who you are and what you can do will forever change your self-image!

YOU'VE GOT WHAT IT TAKES

You already have all the raw material you need for the greatest success you can dream. Consider a common chicken egg. Did you ever stop to think what a wonderful creation it is? That formless, gelatinous mass includes everything necessary for making a baby chick and feeding it until it is large enough to hatch. You look at the egg and see no traces of a beak, legs, bones, eyes, or feathers, but nothing needs to be added to bring this miracle to pass.

Even more astonishing than the potential of an egg is the potential within you to build any kind of future you desire. All that is necessary is to accept the gift of potential that is yours—and then decide to use it.

When a baby chick is strong enough to live outside the shell, it pecks a hole in the shell and begins the job of hatching. If someone tries to help, the chick seldom survives. Likewise, breaking out of your shell is a solo job. *No other person can do it for you.* Sadly, people often look to others to help them, protect them, and even guide them. By doing so, they are short-changing their personal potential. Only God has the wisdom and power to help each of us become all that we are intended to be.

You must initiate the process of hatching. Self-motivation is the sharp beak you use to break out of the shell that limits your full potential. I have seen some people focus on maximizing their potential while others of equal talent and ability choose not to.

> NO SELF-IMAGE WILL EVER BE MAXIMIZED WITHOUT JESUS CHRIST. IT IS SIMPLY IMPOSSIBLE.

To me, it's like two cars at the Texas Motorplex, a drag-racing facility on 500 acres south of Dallas that my son Billy built. When the two cars get the green light, they flash down the track. Often, one of the cars will blow an engine or a tire, and at that moment the remaining car surges ahead, almost as if the damaged car is sitting still.

It's just the same between those who use their full potential and those who do not. By taking charge of your life, you are exercising the initiative to discover the great pool of talents and abilities that make up your inner being. As you remove the padlocks from those qualities that have so far been locked away from your awareness, your full potential will become available.

You have at your disposal the same resources given to any great achiever. Life is an orchestra, and God has given you the baton to direct the interpretation of life's song. You have the same eight notes of the scale that were given to Mozart, Bach, and Chopin.

Life is a painting and you are the artist. You have on your palette all the colors in the spectrum—the same ones available to Michaelangelo and DaVinci. You can choose to use them all, or you can paint your entire life in dull battleship gray.

Life is an adventure story, and you are the writer. You have the same twenty-six letters in the alphabet—the same ones used by Shelley, Milton, and Shakespeare.

You have it all! Use it to its full potential.

PART THREE

BEING TRUE
TO YOURSELF

CHOICES AND CONSEQUENCES

—SAYING "YES" TO ONE
THING MEANS SAYING
"NO" TO ANOTHER

What you choose to say and do will change your life. What's more, it will become your life, affecting you and everyone around you. That is because you possess one of the most powerful forces in the world—the power of choice.

THE FOUR TOP CHOICES IN LIFE

In all of life, there are four basic choices around which the rest of your world will rotate. They are:

1. where you spend eternity

2. whether you discover and pursue your God-given destiny

3. whom you marry

4. how you rear your children

The first choice is simply about whether you have accepted Jesus as your Lord and Savior or not. His death on the cross gives everyone equal access to forgiveness and to God in heaven, but you aren't forced to accept His offer. Where you want to spend eternity is always your choice.

The second choice relates closely to the first. When God says, "I know the plans I have for you, plans to prosper you and not to harm you, plans to give you hope and a future" (Jeremiah 29:11), I believe He means it. However, you still have to make the choice to take Him at His word and then apply yourself to discover what it is He has planned for you. Discovering His purpose for your life, and then living it out, is the most exciting and fulfilling adventure possible!

> YOUR CHOICE IS YOUR POWER.

The third choice receives a lot of attention, and rightly so, since it can positively or negatively affect every area of life. *The choice of a mate is not a decision to be made rashly!* Substantial time needs to be spent in prayer so that you will trust God to bring the perfect mate—the one God has for you—to you at the right time. Until that moment, enjoy life to its fullest!

The final choice is all about how you rear your children. Not long ago a friend confided in me, "The heaviest regret in my life is that I didn't put the quality time into teaching my children my values." He went on to explain, "I depended too much on Sunday school teachers and church leaders. I should have known better, but as someone said, 'We are too soon old and too late smart.'"

In each of these choices, regardless of any factor, we all possess the same power to choose. How wisely you use that power is up to you.

CHOICES HAVE CONSEQUENCES

Making choices will bring consequences, whether good or bad. This may seem a little obvious, but why do people fail to grasp this reality?

The insurance company that fired me when I was young did themselves a great disservice. They said I was shy and introverted when in fact I was purposefully quiet because I was listening and trying to learn from their company's best salesmen, but the manager would not listen to reason and let me go after only three weeks. Within a few short years I was selling circles around their best salesman and could have been a great asset to their company, but it was too late—their "yes" to firing me meant "no" to me ever working for them again.

Consequences, however, are not always bad. Winning an academic scholarship, hitting a sales goal, and making a wise investment might be called "rewards," "profits," or even "luck," but you know otherwise. They are simply consequences for making the right choices.

The Bible calls this principle "sowing and reaping" and says, "A man reaps what he sows" (Galatians 6:7). Whatever it is you plant, whether it is physical, spiritual, mental, financial, relational, or emotional, it will grow and someday come back to you in a multiplied condition. It can be incredibly good or terribly bad—depending on the seed.

> EVERY CHOICE HAS A CONSEQUENCE— AND SINCE IT IS OUR CHOICE, IT IS ALSO OUR RESPONSIBILITY.

LEARN ONE THING, GAIN ANOTHER

When I was a boy, I desperately wanted a bicycle. Instead of buying me one, my dad took me to the junkyard where we selected several old bicycles. We then took the "junk" to our garage where my dad showed me how to strip the bike down to its basic frame. Then he said, "Put it back together and you'll have a bicycle."

Sure enough, when all the parts were reassembled (he made me do it twice), I had a whole bicycle! I even learned how to strip the paint off the metal and repaint it. With the knowledge of how to "make" bicycles, I suddenly found myself with a business opportunity: refurbishing bicycles and selling them. Soon I had bike parts everywhere and "new" bikes for sale. For several years as a teenager I made good money doing this (I refurbished over 300 bicycles!) and loved the confidence and creativity it fostered in me.

Had my father simply bought me a bicycle, I would have missed out on an incredible learning experience. He wanted me to put my first bike together from scratch—and the consequences from that one choice positively impacted my life forever!

By saying "no" to buying a new bicycle, I was saying "yes" to confidence, maturity, creativity, financial gain, and a whole lot more. By saying "yes" to the learning process, I was saying "no" to a welfare I-deserve-it-so-give-it-to-me mentality. We didn't have much money, but *my father showed me that the power of choices and consequences was not bound by the money we did or did not have.* That power was mine, and he showed me how to harness it.

> THE POWER OF CHOICES AND CONSEQUENCES IS NOT BOUND BY THE MONEY YOU DO OR DO NOT HAVE.

In retrospect, he helped unlock in me the potential that I did not see myself. I tried to do the same with my children, though not in exactly the same manner.

I took my five children fishing, hunting, golfing, scuba diving, water skiing, go-cart riding, and more. My son Billy, for example, must have had the best go-cart workshop in the country. He won numerous local competitions as a youngster, and because of his love for speed, he was in professional auto racing for seventeen years.

Being involved in team sports was another passion I tried to instill in my children. As a result, my son Jim went from playing little league baseball to years later coaching a little league baseball team that came within one "out" of making it to the World Series!

According to my priorities, family always came first, regardless of the demands of my work. I've excused myself out of meetings many times in order to spend time with my children. One time I rushed from the office to join my boys in their catamaran and arrived in a suit and tie. As luck would have it, I fell overboard that day, much to my boys' delight!

All told, I've spent more than an hour with my children each day, and I'm so glad I did! It didn't matter if they loved what we did together enough to make a career out of it; I simply wanted to demonstrate my love for them by spending time together. I believe it worked because all five accepted Christ into their lives before their tenth birthday, all have a Christian wife or husband today, and all are actively involved in their church and community.

And the grandchildren? I can't wait to see the impact they will make!

MINOR CHOICES, MAJOR IMPACT

You never know how large the impact may be from a seemingly minor choice. I found this to be the case several years ago on a family vacation when the cruise ship we were on stopped briefly in the Cayman Islands. I asked the captain, "Do you know of any place prettier than this?" He said it was the prettiest of the eight stops the ship would make, so I replied, "OK, we'll get off here."

We spent the rest of our vacation at a condo that was right next door to the house I now own! Little did we know that the Caymans would become the home office to several of our overseas businesses and prove to be one of the best choices we ever made, not to mention the location for many meaningful relationships, unforgettable times as a family, and great business deals. One choice, with many, many positive consequences as a result!

Another time we were flying to Asia and on our stopover in Hawaii I decided to go south rather than take our previously booked flight that went north. We ended up meeting several individuals in Singapore who changed the course of our lives for the better.

> **FOUR MOST IMPORTANT CHOICES IN LIFE**
>
> #1—WHERE YOU SPEND ETERNITY
>
> #2—WHETHER YOU DISCOVER AND PURSUE YOUR GOD-GIVEN DESTINY
>
> #3—WHOM YOU MARRY
>
> #4—HOW YOU RAISE YOUR CHILDREN

Even casual acquaintances can make a big impact in our lives. When I was young and selling insurance to airline pilots, I called on a pilot who was about to move to California. He bought a policy but needed to sell his house and his car quickly, so I bought his Cadillac by getting it financed at a local bank and bought his house by convincing the realtor to loan me the money. My new neighbor happened to be a young pastor by the name of Bill Hinson, who later became one of my best friends and one of the biggest influences in my life.

Not long after, as I was discussing the dissatisfaction of my insurance career with Bill, he told me about a new record company in Waco, Texas, that needed help with its marketing and distribution. I ended up moving to Waco and helped turn the company around—and have lived there ever since!

And if I hadn't moved there, all my children would have married different people and I wouldn't have the grandchildren that I have! In short, I can't even begin to imagine how different my world would be, all because of one choice.

TODAY'S CHOICES BRING TOMORROW'S RESULTS

An elderly Chinese businessman and entrepreneur from Hong Kong, Henry Tseung, flew to Waco to thank me for the impact I had made in his business. Henry was sixty years old and in broken English greeted me with, "You help me, now I help you." Then he explained, "You do day's work; I observe."

So for the entire day, Henry followed me everywhere I went. He listened to my phone calls, observed how I treated personnel, and sat in on my meetings. Part way through the second day, Charles, our sales manager, came into my office to discuss a product. I told Charles almost verbatim what I wanted him to do, say, write, etc. When he left, Henry said, "Henry feel sorry for Charles because he become lesser, lesser person every time he see you."

Neither of us knew the word "empowerment," but in his own way Henry was saying, "You made Charles a puppet. You didn't empower him to be or do anything."

> YOU NEVER KNOW HOW LARGE THE IMPACT MAY BE FROM A SEEMINGLY MINOR CHOICE.

Henry then asked, "Where are company books?" They were in a safe in my office.

He named several other items, all of which were either in my office or somewhere under my close supervision.

"Paul think he can do everything in company better than anybody else," Henry concluded. This may have been true, but I knew business could not grow as fast as it needed to if I did all the work. I had never managed a large company before and didn't know what to do or how to lead it effectively.

I asked, "What do I need to do?"

He replied, "Learn to delegate."

After Henry left, I called in the right people and delegated all the accounting, corporate books, etc., to them. Then I called in the same sales manager and said, "Charles, you are in charge of developing the sales training manuals. If you need ideas, let me know, but otherwise, it's your baby."

My small-business mentality was expanded to fit our enlarging business as I chose to apply the wisdom of Henry's advice. In addition, I learned that you can delegate a job without abdicating authority and that you need to inspect what you expect. My time with the old Chinese businessman was a turning point in my business, but I would have missed it had I made the wrong choice.

The little choices that we encounter on a daily basis may seem trivial, but they also hold the greatest potential for our future. That is because saying "yes" to one thing means saying "no" to another.

THE RISE
AND FALL
OF DISCIPLINE

—IF YOU DON'T HAVE
DISCIPLINE, YOU DON'T
HAVE ANYTHING

The rise and fall of discipline is really the rise and fall of you. That is because discipline plays such an important part in all you do.

A long-time friend of mine, Bernard Rapoport, used to play tennis every morning from 6:30–7:15 on my tennis court. I could set my watch by him. Whether he was finished with a game or not, he would quit at precisely 7:15 and drive directly to his office where he showered, dressed, and was working before 8 A.M.

One day I asked him as he was hurrying to his car, "Why are you so regimented? Why don't you relax a little?"

He looked at me with a you-should-know-better-than-that frown and stated bluntly, "If you don't have discipline, you don't have anything!" With that, he jumped in his car and sped out of my driveway.

I was a little taken aback, but I've come to realize that what he said is exactly right—*if you don't have discipline, you don't have anything!*

DISCIPLINE IS A MUST-HAVE

There are some things in life that would be good to have, like a raise, a better boss, or a Ph.D. Then there are things that you must have, such as food, water, and air. *Discipline ranks in the must-have category, right beside food, water, and air!*

Why? Because if you don't have discipline, no plan, no matter how

> DISCIPLINE IS WHAT YOU NEED TO GET YOU TO WHERE YOU WANT TO GO.

large, great, or cash-generating it is, will ever amount to anything unless someone has the discipline to follow through with it. That is a fact of life.

The great inventor Thomas Edison once explained that the vast majority of his patents and inventions were someone else's—*he was just the one who finished what another had started!* He understood the importance of discipline in everything, whether it was considered important or trivial. It is interesting to note that while in school, Edison was told that he was "too stupid to learn anything." Imagine that!

I was fortunate to be taught discipline as a young man. I learned how to work at a young age, to be on time, to finish what I started, to be dependable, to be

> DISCIPLINE IS NOT SOMEWHERE WAITING TO BE DISCOVERED— *IT IS CREATED.*

organized, and to save a part of all I earned. As a result, I had more money saved at age sixteen than any other teenager I knew! I always disciplined myself to put a portion of my money away in savings. I started this practice at age six and have continued it to this day, never quitting or slacking off.

Discipline is the *process of training* that is designed to produce specific desired patterns of behavior, intended habits, and attitudes that lead to successful performance in various areas of life. In short, *discipline is what you need to get you to where you want to go.*

Success is simply not possible without discipline.

FIVE COMPONENTS OF DISCIPLINE

Where does discipline come from? Discipline isn't somewhere waiting to be discovered—it is created. By combining the following five components of discipline, you will create the discipline you want and need:

> IT IS ONE THING TO PRAISE DISCIPLINE, AND ANOTHER TO SUBMIT TO IT.
>
> —Cervantes

#1—FIRM VALUES

When you know what you believe is right and honorable, you own a set of basic values that are a foundation for directing your choices, decisions, and actions. Such a foundation is a springboard for production in every area of your life.

One pillar in my foundation is Philippians 4:8, which states, "Finally, brothers, whatever is true, whatever is noble, whatever is right, whatever is pure, whatever is lovely, whatever is admirable—if anything is excellent or praiseworthy—think about such things."

By following this one verse, worry, doubt, and insecurity are forced out of my thinking. If it were possible to inspect my inner foundation, no traces of worry, doubt, and insecurity would be found—*simply because they are not there!*

To believe in yourself and what you are doing, you must first overcome any hurdle that might be in your path. Whether it is your environment, habits, or personality, *your decision-making ability preempts them all!* The resulting view of life is what gives you your firm values, which is the basis of your discipline.

Kurt Kaiser, one of the leading composers of Christian music, is a good example of this. He practiced five hours at the piano every day since he was two or three years old. He learned as a child to believe in himself and what he was doing. His dad helped in the process, as Kaiser admits, "My dad would threaten to tie my leg to the piano stool if I didn't play five hours. I cannot remember a day when I did not play five hours."

Kaiser attributes his success today to the discipline he learned as a child.

#2—SETTING CHALLENGING GOALS

God has put within each of us certain dreams and ambitions, as well as the ability to overcome any challenges we might face. However, getting where we want to go will require the discipline of setting and reaching our goals.

Bret Miller is such a person. He went to college to become a doctor. Thousands do it every year, but he was from a poor family and could not afford the tuition. But instead of laying down his dream because of the "impossibility" before him, he pursued it with everything within him. He did what it took to get into school, to stay in school, and then to graduate from school as a doctor. Today he is a successful orthopedic surgeon because of the goals he set and then pursued.

By taking personal responsibility for himself, Bret was saying, "I have a dream within me that will become a reality someday if I do my part to get there." He got there, and inspired others to do the same.

#3—CLEAR PRIORITIES

You have to take the right actions to get the right results. That seems logical enough, but many people don't understand this vital concept because they have undefined priorities.

> "EVERYONE THINKS OF CHANGING THE WORLD, BUT NO ONE THINKS OF CHANGING HIMSELF."
>
> —Tolstoy

Clear priorities are like viewing a mountain range on a crisp, clear winter morning, while having hazy priorities is like viewing the same mountains on a foggy, rainy summer afternoon. Though the mountains are the same, what you see or don't see is vastly different!

So it is with priorities. By keeping up the right actions for the right reasons, you are more likely to maintain the discipline you need and thereby accomplish what it is you have been working toward. One approach to this is preparing yourself to out-serve others. Many business leaders have led their companies to greatness, slowly and purposefully. They knew what they needed to do, and they did it. What some have accomplished would seem impossible at first glance, but with clear priorities, anything is possible!

> "PERSEVERANCE IS BASED ON TWO COMPONENTS: EFFORT AND DESIRE."
>
> —Cal Ripken Jr.

The ant, for instance, is so small and carries with it a seemingly insignificant speck of mortar or food. Yet I have seen ants build or destroy structures of enormous proportions. That is probably why Proverbs says of the ant, "Consider its ways and be wise" (6:6).

The ants start small, but they stay at a single task until it is complete. Clear priorities help bring a single focus by defining your dream and preparing you to hit your goal. Without them, it is far too easy to become distracted and get off track.

#4—PERSISTENCE

The ability to stick with something until it is done is of paramount importance. Sheer persistence has enabled people to claim great accomplishments. Best-selling author and friend Dick Francis is a good example. Every day at the same time he sits down to write, he says, "whether I feel like it or not." His track record speaks for itself: over thirty best-selling books, a new book every year, a personal relationship with the royal family in England, and much more. He understands the power of persistence.

Often those who came in second or third will return next year to win first place. They kept going and won, but where is last year's first place winner? *Winning always comes at the heels of persistence.*

An integral part of persistence is applying yourself to the

goal at hand. Proverbs 23:12 says to *"apply your heart to instruction and your ears to words of knowledge"* (emphasis mine). Mix application with persistence and you have a powerful combination!

Michael Jordan, considered by many to be the best basketball player of all time, was turned down by his high school basketball coach. Jordan wisely asked, "What do I need to do to get on the team?" The coach simply told him that the basics of basketball were required. So Jordan went home and practiced his shooting, dribbling, and passing hour after hour, and the rest is history.

> "PARTIES WHO WANT MILK SHOULD NOT SEAT THEMSELVES ON A STOOL IN THE MIDDLE OF A FIELD IN HOPE THAT THE COW WILL BACK UP TO THEM."
> —Elbert Hubbard

You can do and be anything—if you keep at it.

#5—PERSONAL INSPIRATION

Create your own inspiration because that will truly motivate you. I was turned down by fifty-seven different companies before I finally got my first job selling insurance. By hanging in there, I was finally hired, even though I didn't have the college degree or experience that they required.

Then I worked on my closing average, which was a dismal one out of fourteen. That average continued to decrease while my sales continued to increase. Before long, I was outselling the best salesmen in the company!

> "MAN MUST BE DISCIPLINED, FOR HE IS BY NATURE RAW AND WILD."
> —Immanuel Kant

The more discipline you have, the more "luck" some people will say you have. You know better. Scripture plainly states that "a man reaps what he sows" (Galatians 6:7). I have always seen this as a good thing because I know if I do a good job sowing, I will someday enjoy a bountiful harvest.

Chance occurrences do not happen when you are purposefully trying to do something! When you have a personal drive from within to accomplish your goal, you have results, not accidents.

WHERE THE RUBBER MEETS THE ROAD

The only things in life that do not require discipline are bad habits. It is natural to want to follow the path of least resistance, but to do so is to form a bad habit. Good habits—*the habits you want*—require discipline.

Sadly, most people perform according to their own low expectations. They could be or do absolutely anything they dream of, so why do they settle for anything less? I believe it is because they don't

> "THE GREATEST COMPOSER DOES NOT SIT DOWN TO WORK BECAUSE HE IS INSPIRED, BUT BECOMES INSPIRED BECAUSE HE IS WORKING."
> —Earnest Newman

know what their mission is in life, they don't have a personal relationship with God, and they don't comprehend the power hidden within discipline.

Bernard Rapoport, who told me at precisely 7:15 A.M. that "if you don't have discipline, you don't have anything" hasn't changed a bit. Into his eighties now, Bernard recently bought another company after selling his first company for tens of millions of dollars. His wife told me, "Why stop him—it will add ten years to his life."

Once discipline gets in your system, it becomes a natural part of all you do. That is of utmost importance because if you have discipline, *you can have anything!*

MY WORD
IS MY
BOND

—WHY KEEPING YOUR
WORD IS ABSOLUTELY
INVALUABLE

An employee once came into my office and confided in me, "I don't think I have much longer to live. Would you please make sure my wife is taken care of?"

I was caught completely by surprise. Nothing was wrong with him physically, but for some reason he didn't think he would live much longer. My immediate response was, "Then let's get a life insurance policy on you."

Now it was his turn to think I was joking, but he went ahead and got a policy, naturally passing the physical exam since he was in good health. *Less than ninety days later he was dead from a brain aneurysm!*

Though the company had taken out the life insurance policy, I had made his wife the beneficiary. In addition to that, I paid her half of her husband's regular salary for seventeen years until she was able to get her social security funds. I also had someone manage her insurance money so that it would keep growing and so that she could live in the same house, drive the same type of car, etc.

Why all the effort and expense, even though I wasn't legally bound to lift a finger? Because I chose a long time ago to be a man of my word, regardless of what it might cost me. I had told my friend those many years ago that I would take care of his wife—and I kept my word because my word is my bond.

> THE ONLY THING MORE COSTLY THAN KEEPING YOUR WORD IS NOT KEEPING YOUR WORD.

GET IT IN INK!

Since the 1950s, things have progressively changed. From a handshake to a signed piece of paper to a ten-page document to reams and reams of paper, contracts are not what they used to be.

Every year, people become less and less trusting and more and more suspicious. The increase in the size of contracts—and in the number of lawyers required to explain them—is further indication of the increased lack of trust. Whether it is from greed, dishonesty, mistrust, or as a result of being abused and mistreated, it is sad to see the way the world has changed.

I was not raised that way. Over and over it was pounded into my head to be honest, which always included being:

1. dependable

2. accountable

3. reliable

4. credible

I was taught that you should say what you mean and mean what you say, and that whether you said it or put it in writing, you could be trusted to do what you agreed to do. As a result of being honest, I believe God has honored me, protected me, and blessed me.

KEEPING YOUR WORD HAS ITS PERKS

Though lawyers continue to call me crazy, I keep on "signing" deals with a handshake. Not too long ago I saw a housing complex for sale. I went inside and spoke with the owner. It turned out her husband was sick and in the hospital and they didn't know what to do, didn't understand the tax system, and didn't know how to manage the money if the property did sell. I advised her to give the complex to a local seminary and that the seminary would in turn support her and her husband for the rest of their lives.

She checked into it and agreed to do it, which solved their financial problems, but it meant that I couldn't buy the property. Then six months later the unexpected happened: The seminary called and asked if I would be interested in buying a housing complex they had recently been given. They didn't even know it was the same complex! I bought it by borrowing 100 percent of the money back from the seminary, with two extra points of interest, and a year later sold the complex for 60 percent more than I paid for it!

> WHO STEALS MY PURSE
> STEALS TRASH ...
> BUT HE THAT FILCHES FROM
> ME MY GOOD NAME
> ROBS ME OF THAT WHICH
> NOT ENRICHES HIM,
> AND MAKES ME POOR INDEED.
>
> Shakespeare, Othello

Another time I bought an apartment complex on the back of a lunch place mat for a million dollars and gave the owner $500 cash down. A different time I wrote up a contract on the back of an envelope for a well-known farm in Texas, and with $500 cash down, bought it in front of five realtors and their lawyers who were fighting for the same property! With God's favor, I superceded all of them.

In another instance, I was standing in the lobby of a savings and loan bank when I overheard a discussion about an apartment complex. I said, "It sounds like you have a problem. Can I help you?" One of the men described the complex, then added, *"But we need to get it off our books today!"* We immediately got in a car and raced down to see it. I bought it in five minutes with a handshake, held it six months, sold it, and made $300,000. The man I sold it to was from another state and he sold it six months later and made an additional $600,000 profit.

I've also bought and sold antique cars over the phone, simply trusting the other person's word. People don't usually buy anything without seeing it, but I've sold 70 to 80 percent of my antique cars by telling the other person on the end of the phone to "take my word for it." They haven't been disappointed. With so few people trusting each other these days, I often feel like I'm from a different era, as if I'm one of the last of the Mohicans.

THE VALUE OF KEEPING YOUR WORD

People believe and trust me because I keep my word. They do so not because I say I will do a certain thing, *but because I actually follow through and do what I say I will do.* Intuitively it does not seem that difficult to keep your word, but the increasing number of broken promises proves otherwise.

> KEEPING YOUR WORD TO YOUR CHILDREN IS THE MOST IMPORTANT BUSINESS DEAL POSSIBLE.

Businessman and president of WorkLife Company and Faith@Work ministries,[1] Bill Nix, stated that trust is "the foundation on which our relationships are built. Promise keeping is the adhesive, the substance of our character that prevents the foundation of trust from cracking." He also pointed out in his book *Character Works* that discrimination lawsuits in the workplace have increased by 2,200 percent since 1980! This is the result, I believe, of promises not being kept.

If people forget a promise they made, I do not believe they are in any way excused from keeping their word. Either they should learn not to make a promise they won't keep, or they should write it down and store it for safekeeping. The fact is people don't usually break just one promise—they break many promises.

I take what I say so seriously that I update my will regularly, writing into it the promises that I have made to certain people and marking off the promises that I have fulfilled. I reason that if I can't do what I say I will do, then I have no right to even open my mouth to speak with other people. Not only is my word my bond, but it is a measurement of me as an individual. *If I don't keep my word, then my advice, wisdom, encouragement, counsel, etc., are all suspect.*

> **"A CHRISTIAN'S USEFUL-NESS TO GOD IS DIRECTLY PROPORTIONAL TO HIS HONESTY."**
> —Larry Burkett

What's more, I recognize that to accomplish anything in life, I need other people. If I break my promises, there is no possible way I will reach my goals—it just won't happen. People are vital to every goal and keeping my word to them is of paramount importance.

During a two-week trip several years ago, a friend of mine and I happened to meet seven different young people who all dreamed of going to college. I told each one of them that I would help and that they ought to write me a letter in thirty days telling me what they planned to do with their degrees. Believe it or not, only one of them wrote me! This young lady got her wish—I put her through college—but I never understood why the other six individuals never took me up on my offer. Perhaps they had been burned too many times in the past to believe that I was for real.

Our "yes" should mean "yes" and our "no" should mean "no," just like Jesus stated in Matthew 5:37. Trust, respect, increased business, growth, peace of mind, and much more would come as a result. *Imagine what the world would be like if we all kept our word!*

THE MUTUAL BENEFIT OF KEEPING YOUR WORD

I believe completely that keeping your word is just as beneficial to others as it is to you. A long-time friend of mine Larry Burkett once had a brilliant, highly efficient secretary working for him. When the accounting department needed additional help, Larry transferred her to that department, thinking that she would be a tremendous asset there as well.

However, she performed miserably. Every few minutes she would get a drink, talk to someone, and then slowly return to her desk. Instead of firing her for doing such a poor job, Larry probed a little deeper and found that she hated numbers but loved people. He quickly put her back at the front desk where she blossomed again.

Not long after, another businessman offered her a similar front-desk job that would triple her salary. Larry enthusiastically recommended that she accept the offer, then recommended to her new boss that he always keep her in her area of gifting—to his and her mutual benefit.

That is what keeping your word is all about, and what's more, the benefits often continue for months, years, and even decades!

KEEPING MY WORD—FOR GOOD

When people promise me something, I believe they will do what they say and make a note to remind them in a couple of weeks of their promise. At that point if they say they are not going to follow through on what they promised, I erase from my mind the promise they made. Though disappointed, the fulfilling of the promise rests in their hands, so I release them from it and do not hold it against them. Doing this constantly encourages me to be a man of my word.

> "KEEP YOUR PROMISES EVEN IF OTHERS FAIL IN KEEPING THE PROMISES THEY MAKE TO YOU."
> —Bill Nix

There was a time in my life when it seemed like everyone and everything was against me. The insurance company I worked for went from boom to bust in one weekend when the owners simply walked away, taking every dollar and piece of equipment with them. I could have walked away as well, and was even advised to do so by lawyers, but I chose to stay behind and help put the pieces back together.

When it was all over, I had used over a million of my own hard-earned dollars to fix what I had not broken. At that precise moment I realized that all the money in the world could never be more valuable than my word—*because my word is my bond.*

LEGACY KEY #11

INTEGRITY–
IT'S ALL
YOU ARE

—WHEN ALL YOU HAVE
IS INTEGRITY, YOU HAVE
MORE THAN ENOUGH

At the base of every building is a foundation. Without it, the rain and wind and weather would surely bring the structure to the ground. This is a simple fact of nature that no one questions—it is also hard to argue with a mound of debris.

Similarly, on a personal level, it is not that difficult to see who has built his or her life on a foundation of integrity and who has not. There is a marked difference, and over time, it becomes even more apparent.

INTEGRITY IS WHERE IT ALL BEGINS

Integrity is real and very concrete. It is not what you imagine or wish it to be, like children who cover their eyes with their hands and think they are hiding. *Integrity is very real and very measurable* and includes such traits as:

- taking responsibility

- keeping your word

- being faithful in the little things

- being honest

- standing your ground for what is right

- maintaining your honor and virtue

- being morally upright

- making right choices

- never blaming others

> DO THE RIGHT THING BECAUSE IT'S THE RIGHT THING TO DO.

Integrity is also something you cannot pretend to have. You either have it or you don't, and the new obstacles and opportunities that you face each day will draw out of you what is in you. If your foundation is one of integrity, your decisions will bear that out. If not, that too will become evident.

Many years ago I was selling juice dispensers with plans to get a franchise of my own. But after a month of selling, I discovered some information about the company that undermined my confidence in the product and the franchising possibilities. When I discussed my findings with the owner, he dismissed me as being young, inexperienced, immature, and flat-out wrong.

Instead of doing nothing, I immediately called the individuals I had sold on the product and its franchising potential and recommended that they get a refund since it was still within the three-month trial period. When my boss found out, he was livid and fired me on the spot, but I was on my way out the door anyway.

How could I continue to sell something I didn't believe in? And since I saw holes in the business plan, how could I willingly let other people who trusted me run the risk of losing their money? I couldn't do either of these, so I left the company.

INTEGRITY HAS ITS PRICE

Money would not be the deciding factor as to whether I would be honest or not. Nothing is worth trading your integrity for, even if you stand to lose money, fame, and friendships in the process. I've had:

- businesses dry up instantly with one person's lack of prudence

- people I trusted who then hurt my businesses to a tune of more money than I would ever want to say

- banks unexpectedly call my loans before they were actually due

- fellow Christian businessmen walk away from commitments and leave me holding the bill

Whatever the price, integrity has a greater value. My parents always taught me, "Do the right thing because it's the right thing to do." What I lost as a result of keeping my integrity has always paled in comparison to what I got in return.

> **WITH INTEGRITY AS THE BEDROCK FOUNDATION, THE HEIGHT AND WIDTH OF WHAT ANY OF US BUILD IS NEVER LIMITED.**

If I lost a sale by being honest, I gained it back by making a bigger sale because of my honesty. If I allowed coworkers to have the limelight instead of me, I benefited by having the highest caliber of leaders to manage my companies. If I lost friendships because I stood up for what was right, the friends I lost were not really friends in the first place—they would have done me more harm than good. If I lost money by keeping my word to an employee, I gained employees who trusted and respected me enough to work for me for twenty and thirty years!

In all honesty, everything I think I ever lost or might have lost by choosing integrity was really not a loss at all. Proverbs 20:21 says, "An inheritance quickly gained at the beginning will not be blessed at the end." I believe that what I could have gained would have been only temporary at best, bringing long-term hurt in the end.

But desiring to be a person of integrity does not make you perfect. Ever since I asked Jesus into my heart, my desire has been to obey God and honor Him with my life, but I haven't always made the right moves. I've tipped the boat of life over several times, but God has always forgiven me and given me an opportunity for a fresh start.

Sometimes the fresh start meant rebuilding from the foundation again, but at least the foundation was there! Integrity is the bedrock upon which anything can stand, no matter how high you go.

There were times when I literally had nothing left but my integrity. It was *not* easy, but for my character and for my future, it did wonders! At one point an incredible business deal I had worked hard to line up was stopped dead in the water at the last minute because I refused to pay a bribe. I was as good as broke at that stage in my life, but I clung to my integrity. Only a few weeks later the value of keeping my integrity became evident.

INTEGRITY HAS ITS REWARDS

> EVERY TIME I FELT THE ONLY THING I POSSESSED WAS MY INTEGRITY, I DISCOVERED THAT I STILL HAD PLENTY.

With my business venture down the drain because I refused to pay a bribe, I was ready for something new. I chose to work for a record company that needed help in its sales and marketing division. Plans for starting my own company were brewing, but I first needed experience in the recording industry.

One year before I was planning on launching Success

Motivation Institute (SMI), I was suddenly fired after a stellar year, simply because I was making more money through commissions than the management was! I jumped straight into SMI with all I had: my integrity, very limited cash, and a whole lot of vision.

SMI began to grow, but before long we were in a tight spot financially. I flew to New York to meet with a large business owner who liked what we were offering. He said I had a guaranteed sale on the condition that we take out every reference to anything spiritual from our materials.

I replied, "Well, I guess I just missed a sale." That sale was extremely important to us and would have been the boost we needed as a company to make ends meet, but undermining my integrity was something I would not do. On the return flight, I cried most of the way home— *but the story didn't end there!*

> "TRY NOT TO BECOME A PERSON OF SUCCESS, BUT RATHER A PERSON OF VALUE."
>
> —Albert Einstein

When I walked into my office there was a letter waiting for me; an insurance company in the Midwest wanted to know if I would come and speak to their key managers in their sales department. I called and said they would not have to pay me if they would let me have a few minutes to offer our sales programs to the eighty-seven managers in attendance. They agreed, so I immediately loaded a truck with eighty-seven of our sales courses.

My mind was already made up. *I was going to sell 100 percent of those in attendance!* I also *needed* to sell them to pay our bills, and that only made me even more determined. When it came time to make a sales presentation, the atmosphere was almost electric—and I sold all eighty-seven programs!

I didn't know it at the time, but Charles Roth, author of more than twenty-seven books on selling, happened to be an invited guest and was in the room that day. I might have been distracted had I known he was there, but I was so focused on making the sale that nothing could have interrupted my concentration. Years later, he wrote in one of his books that my sales presentation that day was the best he had ever witnessed in his entire life.

By selling all eighty-seven programs, we got the boost our company so desperately needed. I believe God honored me for turning down the sure business deal in New York and sticking to my convictions. Proverbs says,

- *"The integrity of the upright guides them, but the unfaithful are destroyed by their duplicity"* (11:3).

- *"The man of integrity walks securely, but he who takes crooked paths will be found out"* (10: 9).

- *"Righteousness guards the man of integrity, but wickedness overthrows the sinner"* (13:6).

Since that time, SMI and many other companies I started have grown by leaps and bounds. *With integrity as the bedrock foundation, the height and width of what any of us build is never limited.* The sky is truly the limit!

Here are just a few of the rewards I have experienced for keeping integrity:

- increased sales and profits

- long-tenured employees

- inspiration and motivation

- protection and security

- unexpected favor

- respect and appreciation

- profitable ideas for new businesses

- a good name and reputation

- opportunity to be a role model and mentor

- optimum health

- great friendships

- satisfaction from achieving my goals

- peace and contentment

- God's blessings in every part of my life

- childlike excitement for the future

Integrity is for winners, and winners always win. History agrees; the good guys always win in the end.

INTEGRITY—ARE YOU BOUND TO IT?

By its very essence, integrity requires faithfulness, honesty, obedience, and more. There have been times when I've refunded people out of my own pocket for things that I was not responsible for. Was I legally bound to do so? Not at all, but being legally bound is not the point.

Laws were designed to complement or back up what we already do on a personal level, not force us into action. For example, individuals who refuse to pay child support until they are about to lose their driver's license or be thrown in jail are really being controlled by the law. If they had personal integrity, the need for getting the police involved would never have occurred.

> "THE FINEST LUXURY OF LIFE IS INTEGRITY OF MIND AND SPIRIT."
> —Jim Cole

Similarly, businesspeople who complain when you stand up for what is right or who train their sales team to be less than honest are really undermining the whole basis of business and sales: trust, respect, and honor.

Does integrity bind and restrict or does it bring freedom and peace? It is constricting to those who don't want to do what is right, while it is freeing to those who recognize the benefits of being a person of integrity. That is because integrity, at its foundation, is an issue of the heart.

In your journey of life, if you ever find yourself with nothing left but your integrity, *then you have more than enough!*

PART FOUR

MY WORK
IS MY
MINISTRY

MY WORK
IS MY
MINISTRY

—FREEDOM COMES
WHEN THEY ARE
ONE AND THE SAME

My work and my ministry are the same as far as I am concerned. Nowhere in Scripture does it say that God differentiates between work and ministry, secular and sacred. Instead, He says, "Whatever you do, whether in word or deed, do it all in the name of the Lord Jesus" (Colossians 3:17).

Noted speaker and author of *Man in the Mirror*,[2] Patrick Morley, made it plain when he said, "The issue isn't whether or not you are in ministry, but whether or not you are faithful in the ministry God has given you."

This is vitally important! If we are not faithful in our work because we are yearning to be "in the ministry," then we are doing a disservice to God, ourselves, and to everyone we meet. In fact, "if you have not been trustworthy with someone else's property, who will give you property of your own?" (Luke 16:12).

I believe this means that until we are faithful where God places us, we will not be released to do what we have always dreamed of doing. Honestly answering the question, "What is my motive for wanting to be in ministry?" is a good place to start.

FINDING MUCH-NEEDED PEACE

A lot of dissatisfied people will find peace with God and themselves when they come to grips with the fact that doing what God has equipped and enabled them to do is most important, regardless of what or where that might be.

When I was twenty-four years old and excelling in the insurance business, I was invited to a meeting with about twenty of North America's most influential preachers and speakers. In comparison to them, I felt like the only talent I had was making money. One of the men looked at me and said, "Paul, God's will for your life might be to make money. You just need to be obedient to do what He has equipped and enabled you to do; *that is* your ministry."

His comment brought great liberty to my heart and soul. I was free from thinking that I should be doing something more "meaningful." Instead, I could focus on what God had for me to do. (Making money, it turned out, was only a small part of what God had planned for me.)

Once and for all, we need to put to rest the notion that the only way to please God or to make an impact in the world is to be a minister of the gospel. Our work is not something we

> "95 PERCENT OF US WILL NEVER BE IN 'OCCUPATIONAL' MINISTRY, BUT THAT DOES NOT MEAN WE ARE NOT MINISTERS."
> —Patrick Morley

do in hopes that we will have an opportunity to do ministry; it is ministry! God has called us to work. People who have been searching for their divine calling might find it has been under their noses all along.

THE EXCITING THRILL OF WORK

According to one survey reported in *Business Week* magazine, only one out of six Americans is content with his or her job, which means nearly 83 percent are dissatisfied! How can people live like that?

Should they quit, get another job, or go into business for themselves? Some ought to, but most won't. They will stay in their current position out of need, fear of change, lack of vision, or some other debilitating reason.

Many years ago I was asked to visit a twenty-six-year-old man who was hospitalized with bleeding ulcers. After briefly getting acquainted, I looked him in the eye and asked, *"If you had nobody to please in life, what would you do?"*

> "YOUR WORK SHOULD BE A CHALLENGE, NOT A CHORE; A BLESSING, NOT A BORE."
>
> —Hal Stevvins

He immediately started to cry like a child. Through tears, he sobbed, "I have always wanted to be a farmer."

Instead of pursuing his lifelong passion, he was in college working toward a degree he knew he didn't want to use! It was a nightmare for him, each day enduring a life he hated living. He was a square peg in a round hole —the proverbial fish out of water—to a degree that I had never witnessed before!

I told him he needed to call in his family who loved him and who were concerned about him, but who thought they knew what was better for his life than he did, and tell them he could no longer live the life they were planning for him. Out of a misshapen sense of obedience and love for his parents and family, he was trying so hard to be somebody he was not. But it was his life and he wanted to be the one writing the story.

I admired his courage as I watched him, with tears streaming down his face, tell his family what had been on his heart for so many years, *and they finally understood!*

Having made that decision, the healing process began

immediately. The doctor attending him was also a friend of mine and told me that within twenty-four hours of the family confrontation, the young man's ulcers suddenly stopped bleeding! Until then the ulcers were out of control—the doctors had tried everything and nothing could stop the bleeding! In no time at all, the young man walked out of the hospital, never to return to the hospital or to any college campus again.

Today he is a farmer, owns a feed store, has a wife and kids, and is living a life he always wanted to live. I consider him to be one of the richest men I have ever known, not for the fact that he makes a lot of money, but for the fact that he is pursuing his life's dream and calling.

> "I NEVER REMEMBER FEELING TIRED BY WORK, THOUGH IDLENESS EXHAUSTS ME COMPLETELY."
>
> —Sir Arthur Conan Doyle

Meeting that day with him was an experience for both of us. He discovered what it meant to be free from the suffocating demands and expectations of other people and I realized afresh that I love doing what I do. *For me, work is pure joy!*

Another time I was in a subway in New York when I sat beside a businessman. He was a stockbroker and living the big life, but I intrigued him when I mentioned the power and importance of goal setting and having the right priorities. He ended up buying one of my programs before we reached his station.

That night he wrote down everything he wanted to do in life. When he was done, he said to his wife, "I just realized I'm not doing anything I really want to do."

After further thought and with his wife's support and encouragement, he quit his job and moved to Colorado. There he put together a group of investors and went into the oil business. He drilled thirteen dry holes, one after the other, but not one of the investors backed out (He was a powerful motivator and businessman to keep them together!). Then, on the fourteenth hole, he hit the jackpot and hit about twenty more in a row after that.

Though he is a multimillionaire today, his satisfaction comes from doing what he has always wanted to do. My satisfaction is in the fact that if he hadn't bought my program, he probably would not have made such a pivotal move with his family.

How many other people are in careers or in college who don't belong there? Will each of us be able to say to God, "I used the talents and abilities that You gave me to their fullest potential"? Granted, there is often a season when you have to do what you have to do, but not forever and certainly not when it goes against your morals, values, priorities, and skills!

For me, work is as thrilling as it is fulfilling. My work is my ministry, and as a result, I have determined that I will:

1. Set a good example through what I do

2. Combine faith with my works

3. Keep ministry as priority

#1

SETTING AN EXAMPLE THROUGH WHAT I DO

How we work is the best example of who we really are on the inside. Add in the ingredient of money, however, and people's ethics often turn into "situational ethics."

My friend Bill Nix knows this only too well. When he was an investment banker, he was once poised to make two million dollars on a 500 million-dollar construction project. Everything was on target until a representative from the bank handling the money called to ask for $10,000 in cash to "make sure everything worked smoothly." Bill knew

> GOD DOES NOT PRACTICE SITUATIONAL ETHICS BECAUSE HE IS "THE SAME YESTERDAY AND TODAY AND FOREVER" (HEBREWS 13:8), AND NEITHER SHOULD WE.

it was a bribe and said he wouldn't do it. The phone went dead and the deal stopped cold.

For Bill, two million dollars wasn't enough to waiver on his ethics. No price was high enough because he had decided long ago that he would remain true to God's Word, regardless of the situation or size of the check. Those who practice situational ethics have yet to make this decision in their hearts.

History reveals that Sir Arthur Conan Doyle once played a practical joke on twelve respected and well-known men whom he knew. He sent out twelve telegrams with the same message on each: "Flee at once. All is discovered."

Within twenty-four hours, they had all left the country!

Each of these men obviously had something to hide. Suddenly, though only in jest, the cover had been pulled away to reveal their true nature—and they fled. Such a lifestyle is not a legacy I would want to leave behind.

Some time ago, one of the buildings I owned was damaged in a hailstorm. The insurance company didn't want to pay our insurance claim and decided to send a representative to my town to check up on me. When he arrived, he spoke with one of our company presidents who said, "Why don't you drive around Waco and talk to bankers and business owners and see what they say about Paul J. Meyer?"

So for the rest of the afternoon the insurance representative drove from business to bank, asking questions about my integrity and business ethics. When he returned he said to our company president, "You can't beat Jack Armstrong in his own backyard!"

That was his way of acknowledging that I was indeed a man of principle, as several business owners and bankers must have testified. Scripture says, "Every tree is known by its own fruit" (Luke 6:44 NKJV), and what the insurance man discovered about me that afternoon was an accurate reflection of me as a person. And the same day the insurance company decided to pay our entire claim!

#2
COMBINING FAITH WITH WORKS

When it comes right down to it, good works without faith aren't worth anything—*at least from God's perspective!* We, on the other hand, are masters at making what we do of such great importance that we lose sight of this reality.

> "WHAT GOOD IS IT, MY BROTHERS, IF A MAN CLAIMS TO HAVE FAITH BUT HAS NO DEEDS?"
> —James 2:14

For centuries, mankind has tried in vain to gain right standing with God by doing good works. This work-your-way-to-heaven approach is the basis for many religions, but that is not the case for Christianity. If it were, then there would have been no need for Jesus to die on the cross, but Jesus *did* die on the cross for our sins so that through faith we could have our relationship with our Father in heaven restored.

We gain nothing with God through good works because "it is *by grace* you have been saved, through faith . . . *not by works*" (Ephesians 2:8–9, emphasis mine). Good works by themselves will lead to legalism, bondage, and death, while faith by itself is little more than hot air.

Combine the two and:

- God's will is accomplished through you

- people's lives are changed

- you are changed

- life takes on a whole new meaning

- excitement and fresh vision come in abundance

Not long ago I read about a boy in our local newspaper who needed very expensive surgery. His parents could not afford the operation, much less the flight to the special hospital in Houston. So, I spoke with several doctors and they agreed to operate at no charge. Then I chartered a plane and flew the boy to Houston for the five-hour surgery. All this was to give him a fighting chance at having a normal life.

The mother said to me soon after, "I have heard of people helping other people, but I've never seen it with my own eyes."

I was saddened by what she said, but it made me realize once again how meaningful a kind act can be. It also made me see more clearly how good deeds with a pure motive will point directly to God, while deeds done to get "brownie points" with God always point back to one's self. I helped her son because of my burning desire to bless other people, a decision that is based on my extreme appreciation for what God has done for me.

I recognize that I am also responsible to do good works, as James 4:17 NKJV explains, "To him who knows to do good and does not do it, to him it is sin." This, I believe, is because God has plans for each one of us, things that He can only accomplish through us. Scripture says that we were created "to do good works, which God prepared in advance for us to do" (Ephesians 2:10).

I read that Abraham Lincoln was once strolling through town when he saw a slave girl being sold at auction. He entered the bidding and purchased the girl. Her first question to her new master was "What are you going to do with me?"

Lincoln replied, "Set you free."

When she realized that she could do what she wanted, wear what she wanted, say what she wanted, and go where she wanted, she was speechless. Lincoln asked her, "What are you going to do now?"

She immediately replied, "Go with you."

> "FEW CHRISTIANS WHO VIEW THEIR WORK AS A CHORE HAVE MUCH OF A WITNESS ON OR OFF THE JOB."
>
> —Larry Burkett

Not only does her comment reveal that she was pretty smart—choosing to align herself with someone who was just, kind, and merciful—but it also reveals the power of doing what is right. Instead of complaining, arguing, or making a commotion at the auction, Lincoln simply took action. He did so, I believe, because his work was his ministry.

#3
KEEPING MINISTRY AS THE PRIORITY

One of my business priorities is to support local ministries and organizations with revenues brought into our family's companies. The employees, I always tell them, play a vital part in this as well because we could not do all we do without them. We are working together to the benefit of our local community.

But giving money is not the only way we can show where our priorities lie. Several years ago I met a man who was facing increased health problems and a business that he could not handle. With only a meager retirement, he was in trouble.

I advised him how to use his business to fund his retirement. That much-needed advice proved to be the answer to his dilemma and he is now retired and financially set for the rest of his life.

All it cost was a little of my time and attention. Had I been focused solely on money, I would have missed the opportunity to positively impact another person's life.

When I see work as my ministry, I willingly put others first and me second. That is what service is all about. In every situation, we must ask ourselves, "What is my priority?" I have canceled meetings to speak with people who needed urgent help, given thousands of dollars to help meet bills, mortgages, and car payments for complete strangers, and written hundreds of letters, notes, and faxes to people who needed encouragement. By doing these and other things, I am demonstrating what my priorities are.

THE BOTTOM LINE WHEN WORK IS MINISTRY

There have been times when I've been invited to speak and right before I go on stage the coordinator pulls me aside and says, "Don't mention Jesus or God, OK? We don't want to offend anyone."

I always smile and thank them, then get on stage and tell the audience that when I listen to people speak, I always want to know from what basis they are supporting their beliefs, principles, and advice. Then I tell them that my beliefs are based on God and His Word. As a listener, I would expect nothing less.

> **WHEN WORK IS OUR MINISTRY, OTHERS ARE FIRST AND WE ARE SECOND.**

It is important that everyone have the same chance I did to reach their full potential, and I believe *without Jesus Christ, it is impossible that they ever will.*

This view has sparked countless debates, letters to the editor in local newspapers, phone calls, discussions, rebukes, and more. *Newsweek* magazine even called me a "jug-eared evangelist" on account of my big ears and what I said from stage, but it doesn't matter to me. My sincere hope is that someone will come to the freeing, saving, and incredible knowledge of Jesus Christ through what I do and what I say.

That is the bottom-line reason why my work is my ministry.

IT'S ALL HIS BY RIGHT OF CREATION

—DISCOVERING THE JOY
AND RESPONSIBILITY
OF STEWARDSHIP

W hen I fly over a city, I often think of the courthouse with
its records of who owns which parcel of the thousands
of little pieces of land. People have their name on a deed and
think they own the land, but they don't, not even for a minute!
In less than 100 years, not a single person will own an inch of
it—*someone else will own it all!*

People give their entire lives to get a deed or attain a certain level of wealth, and then they leave without it. It is such a
waste, but before we feel bad about believing the same lie ourselves, consider the fact that many of us:

- grew up watching our parents pass like ships in the night,
  one leaving for work just as the other returned from work.

- watched one or both of our parents climb the financial
  Mount Everest where halfway up they forgot who they
  were, what their priorities were, where they were going,
  whom they were married to, what promises they had
  made, etc.

♦ witnessed the person with the nicer clothes, bigger house, or faster car receive preferential treatment, even from our parents.

We learned through observation what was "right" and "normal," but sadly we were never told there was more to the picture.

STEWARDSHIP—NOT WHAT WE ARE USUALLY TAUGHT

A steward is someone who manages what belongs to another person. Because God created the universe, everything is His by right of creation. As objects of His creation, we are stewards at best and never owners.

This reality affects us in every area, from our finances to our time and from our abilities to our children. Everything has all been entrusted to us by God. Scripture says, "The earth is the LORD's, and everything in it, the world, and all who live in it" (Psalms 24:1) and "Every good and perfect gift is from above" (James 1:17). This does not leave much for us to claim credit for, does it?

Why is stewardship so important? Because everyone who does not accept the position that we are stewards will fall far short of fulfilling God's will for his or her life, even to the point of stalling or quitting altogether. We cannot honor God or fully achieve any goal when we believe we are owners.

> HOW MUCH OR HOW LITTLE WE HAVE IS NOT NEARLY AS IMPORTANT AS WHAT WE DO WITH IT.

Why is stewardship so important to me? Part of the answer is my mother—what she *said* and what she *did*. When I was in my twenties and doing very well in the insurance business, she visited me in Miami and saw my home, my car, and other material possessions. She looked me in the eye and said, "Paul, I am frightened by your early success. Don't forget who gave you the talent, don't forget who owns it all, and don't let

Satan use your success to take you away from what's important." I never forgot her words, but what she did many years later changed my life.

In 1969, she fell in her home and wasn't found for two days (she died a few days later in the hospital with me holding her hand). In the apron she was wearing the day she fell, I found a note that read: "S.S. HOPE: 7 miles, 7 cents." I cried uncontrollably, realizing that she had raised seven cents after walking seven miles for S.S. HOPE,[3] a hospital ship that provided medical care to people in developing nations. Those seven miles might have even been what killed her. Her example was the most powerful act of stewardship I have ever witnessed!

EIGHT PILLARS OF STEWARDSHIP

Of the many important stewardship qualities, I believe there are eight foundational pillars that bring strength, wealth, balance, and permanence to individuals who recognize their role is that of a steward.

PILLAR #1—PAYING GOD FIRST WITH THE TITHE

Tithing is only one aspect of stewardship, but I don't believe I am a good steward unless I pay my tithe. Tithing (paying God 10 percent off the gross) is an integral part of stewardship because it accomplishes three primary objectives:

1. It says who is Lord of your life. ("You cannot serve both God and Money," Matthew 6:24)

2. It requires you to walk by faith. ("Without faith it is impossible to please God," Hebrews 11:6)

3. It allows God to bless you. ("Then your barns will be filled to overflowing, and your vats will brim over with new wine," Proverbs 3:10)

I started tithing at age twenty-seven and was proud about it, thinking that my 10 percent to God was pretty impressive. Around that time my pastor, Bill Hinson, invited me to a speech by businessman and philanthropist Robert G. LeTourneau. That night LeTourneau stated that *he gave away 90 percent of his income and lived on the remaining 10 percent!* I left the meeting and said to Bill, "So much for my arrogance on my 10 percent!"

I decided right then that I would learn to give more and rely on God more—*and the more I gave, the more He gave me in return!* My path of learning, however, was not an easy road. Six months after I started tithing, I lost 90 percent of my net worth due to a business fiasco that I was not responsible for. In turning to God for answers, I found that the first half of Malachi 3:10 says to "bring the whole tithe into the storehouse, that there may be food in my house." It does not say anything about bringing the tithe "when you can afford it" or paying it "with whatever is left over." Paying the tithe is simply a principle of stewardship, whether you have a lot of money or not.

> "I BELIEVE THAT EVERY RIGHT IMPLIES A RESPONSIBILITY; EVERY OPPORTUNITY, AN OBLIGATION; EVERY POSSESSION, A DUTY."
> —John D. Rockefeller Jr.

I tell people who ask for financial advice, "If you aren't tithing, then my counsel will do you no good. We are to pay our tithes first, then our taxes and bills." With perplexed looks, they often reply, "We are not paying our bills now; how are we supposed to start tithing?"

The only time God ever challenges us to test Him in the entire Bible is in the area of tithing! He said in the last half of Malachi 3:10 to "test me in this and see if I will not throw open the floodgates of heaven and pour out so much blessing that you will not have room enough for it."

When I lost 90 percent of my income, I continued to tithe. Did God immediately pour out on me more blessings than I could contain? *No, things actually went from bad to worse!* But before long, things began to change, doors began to open, and fresh vision began to come. Where I ended up, both geographically and career wise, could only have come from God!

Those in financial straits who start tithing are also the ones who have the discipline to live within their means, change their lifestyle, and reduce their debts. Many times their tithing brings miraculous results, other times it's more gradual, but whatever happens in the short-term, when they are obedient to God's command, they will discover that God *always* keeps His promises.

PILLAR #2—KEEPING COMMITMENTS EVEN WHEN IT HURTS

When President Reagan changed the tax laws on real estate in the early 1980s, I again found myself in a financially difficult position. I had committed to give a certain amount each month to several Christian organizations, but suddenly I was losing that same amount every month!

I sold properties and even took out loans to keep the commitments I had made. Bankers thought I was crazy, but I knew God would take care of me because His Word clearly states, "Give, and it will be given to you. A good measure, pressed down, shaken together and running over, will be poured into your lap. For with the measure you use, it will be measured to you" (Luke 6:38).

What happened? Exactly what the Scripture said would happen! The measure I used was given back to me and I was able to keep every one of my commitments. Was it quick and easy? No, but God kept His promise and provided for me, even when things looked impossible. My

> "ALL THE MONEY IN THE WORLD IS NO USE TO A MAN OR HIS COUNTRY IF HE SPENDS IT AS FAST AS HE MAKES IT. ALL HE HAS LEFT IS HIS BILLS AND THE REPUTATION FOR BEING A FOOL."
>
> —Kipling

financial books at the time revealed that whenever a commitment was due, my income increased, and in months when a commitment was not due, my income dropped!

I may never be required to give as sacrificially as my mother did, but Scripture commands, "If anyone has material possessions and sees his brother in need but has no pity on him, how can the love of God be in him? Dear children, let us not love with words or tongue but with actions and in truth" (1 John 3:17–18). It does *not* say we have to first be financially well off.

PILLAR #3—FINANCIAL RESPONSIBILITY

Each of us is financially responsible for what we have control over. This means at the very least that God expects interest on what He gives us. The servant who buried his master's talent of gold instead of investing it was told, "You should have put my money on deposit with the bankers, so that when I returned I would have received it back with interest" (Matthew 25:27). I believe God desires, for our sake and His, that we multiply whatever He entrusts to us.

Does that mean we can never make mistakes? Of course not! I've lost money in investments and had numerous businesses close their doors. Am I a bad steward as a result? Not in the slightest! Winning over the long haul is what matters, which means setbacks are never the end of the road.

Scripture encourages me when it declares, "I was young and now I am old, yet I have never seen the righteous forsaken or their children begging bread" (Psalm 37:25). The righteous

> GIVING, AT ITS CORE, IS A HEART ATTITUDE.

have a promise that extends beyond fluctuations in the stock market and economic downturns! However, if an investment or business is going down the drain, chasing bad with good is not an act of good stewardship.

I once found a prime piece of real estate for sale; the only problem was that it was owned by a person with a somewhat unsavory business reputation. When he offered me the property, I did a little footwork of my own (as is my usual case) and quickly discovered that all of his deals were not on the up-and-up.

Though I really wanted the property, I proceeded slowly and carefully. I had my attorney draft a comprehensive earnest-money deposit contract, with the final draft being much larger than the customary five or six pages.

The property owner signed the document, but I had difficulty getting him to close. He kept stalling for one reason or another, hoping I would back out of the deal. After a couple of months passed, I called him and asked if he was ready to close on our contract. I also asked if he understood what the word "checkmate" meant. He had no way of legally backing out of the contract—he knew it and his lawyer knew it. "Let's close the deal," I said, then hung up the phone, knowing the property would be mine in a few days, *and it was!*

Had I played by his rules, I would have lost my deposit and missed a great opportunity. Instead, I guarded my investment by due diligence and preparing myself and I came out the winner. Scripture says to "be as shrewd as snakes and as innocent as doves" (Matthew 10:16). That piece of property is one of the best real estate investments I ever made, selling several years later for five times what I paid for it!

PILLAR #4—BEING A NONSTOP GIVER

A giver will always give, regardless of how much or how little he or she might have. That is because giving, at its core, is an attitude of the heart. Being a giver, however, does take effort. Everything will be tested, including:

- ◆ your trust in God

- ◆ your moral fiber

- ◆ your commitment to honor pledges in faith that God will supply the means to pay them

- ◆ your ability to internalize the truth that God will supply every one of your needs

Charlie "Tremendous" Jones said it perfectly when he said, "You can't really enjoy anything without sharing it, and this includes your faith, love, talents, and money. Someday you'll discover we never really give; we are only returning and sharing a small portion of what we've received."

And no matter how much you give, God will never allow you to give Him more than He gives back to you—*never!*

PILLAR #5—BE FAITHFUL WITH WHAT YOU HAVE

People who complain or wish they had what other people have *are not being good stewards over what God has entrusted to them.* Most of the time God gives seemingly small opportunities—we take it from there. Scott Preissler, CEO of Christian Stewardship Association, wrote me a note once that read, "My dad served Ford Motor Company for thirty-three years in a very large manufacturing factory. He took me there often and that experience helped me see what 'alternative options' there might be for me if I did not pursue my own goals."

> "YOU MAKE A LIVING BY WHAT YOU GET . . . BUT YOU MAKE A LIFE BY WHAT YOU GIVE."
>
> —Winston Churchill

Scott knew where his life was headed if he did not take control of it. When opportunities came his way, he took them and, as a result, ended up in a career that both fulfills and excites him.

John Cook, a long-time friend and business associate, did not have the opportunities that Scott had. John was diagnosed with polio soon after his first child was born and the doctors said he would be on an iron lung for the rest of his life, but he and his wife believed otherwise. Within no time he was off the machine and within two years he was 90 percent restored! I was fortunate to hire him as my first employee.

John understood that he had to make the best of what life

presented. He refused to give up, quit, or be defeated and was an inspiration to everyone he met. When he died in the fall of 2000, the world lost one of the best stewards of talents and abilities I have ever known. He could take the seemingly impossible and turn it into something great! Such is the mentality of a steward.

> "GOD LOVES A CHEERFUL GIVER."
> —2 Corinthians 9:7

PILLAR #6—STEWARDS TRAIN OTHERS

Stewards multiply themselves by training other people to be good stewards. This is especially effective with children. Howard Dayton, CEO of Crown Financial Ministries,[4] says that children need training in four distinct areas, including the establishing of routine responsibilities, exposure to work, earning extra money at home, and working for other people.

I taught my children early the concept of tithing, giving, saving, and investing. What they did with my advice and training was up to them, but I am happy to say that each of them has made wise investments for their families here on earth and for their futures in heaven. They in turn have taught their children the same principles of stewardship!

To foster this attitude with my grandchildren, at times I will give them gifts in the form of animals that Heifer Project International[5] then gives to needy families around the world. My grandkids receive a picture of the animal, its name, and where it is going. What they quickly realize is that each animal is a blessing to other people in need *and that the gift will continue to multiply for generations!*

PILLAR #7—OBEDIENCE AND TRUST TOWARD GOD

Stewardship is often condensed into time, talent, and treasure, but I believe there is one more ingredient: my testimony.

Being a good steward has everything to do with my relationship with Jesus Christ. Do I trust Him? Am I willing to obey Him? *Both questions will be answered in the way I handle my finances.*

As a steward it is my responsibility to simply do what He says to do (the outcome is therefore His responsibility). The rich young ruler in the Bible who went away sad when Jesus asked him to give away his wealth failed to understand that his obedience and trust toward God were all he had to offer—*the wealth he "owned" was already God's!*

When we give our obedience and trust to God, the doors of blessing open wide, so much so that we will not be able to contain it all. God always does "immeasurably more than all we ask or imagine" (Ephesians 3:20). For some rea-

> **YOUR HEART IS WHERE YOUR MONEY IS.**
> —Matthew 6:21, paraphrased

son, this principle of obeying God and trusting Him to provide is something we hear very little about.

Several years ago I was asked to speak at Saint Andrews University in Scotland to the students, staff, and a large number of local pastors. I began by stating that I wanted to take everyone's stewardship pulse. They were a little puzzled until I asked them to take out their checkbooks and show me what they did with their money over the past ninety days. "It will tell me where your heart is," I explained.

Of course I didn't look at their checkbooks, but they were stunned nonetheless—*and it made them think.* Several of the pastors came up to me afterward and said, "What you said needs to be preached from every pulpit in the nation. If it were, churches would be radically different from what they are today."

Our hearts are where our money is. The reality of this fact cannot be swept under the carpet—after all, it is our testimony we are talking about.

PILLAR #8—ALWAYS ROOM FOR IMPROVEMENT

Paul Piper, a highly successful businessman and friend of mine for many years, says that learning from others in the area of stewardship and finances is an absolute must. Though he passed the eighty-year-old mark a while ago, he still considers himself to be a student.

Before I had even started tithing, Paul and his wife Katy had already set up their first foundation with the express purpose of funding the kingdom of God. Their two boys were young and the Pipers wanted them to be "trained in Christian charity as much as in business."

The Pipers are such givers that I thought, "If they can do it, so can I." Their example has encouraged me to increase my giving by 500 percent! They also understand the joy of giving like no other couple I know.

THE JOY OF GIVING

What makes being a good steward such a joy? Is it the fact that you have something to be a steward with? Is it that you are able to manage it wisely? Is it that God has found you faithful with financial wealth?

All of these to some degree, but my greatest joy comes from giving it away. I once met a woman who was sacrificing her life, money, and time for the benefit of little children. When she explained what she was doing, I promised to help fund her dream. She was so excited and thankful that she started to cry! Now past age seventy, she is still going strong because she has so much vision and excitement for serving and giving to other people. Giving to her brought tremendous joy, so much so that *I don't believe you can truly experience joy if you don't give your money away.*

> "IF WE WORK OUR FINGERS TO THE BONE, PINCH AND SAVE EVERY PENNY FOR A RAINY DAY, WHO KNOWS, BEFORE NO TIME AT ALL WE MAY BE THE RICHEST PERSON IN THE CEMETERY."
> —Carl C. Wood

Patrick Morley, author, businessman, and president of a

charitable organization, has dealt with wealthy businessmen for decades. His condensed insight is this: "The greater proportion of a man's income he gives, the happier he is."

No joy matches my joy from giving. I've told wealthy businesspeople, "You thought it was fun making it. Well, you don't know what fun is until you start giving it away." Many have come to me later with a bounce in their step and a smile from ear to ear and said, "It's true!"

I tell Jane, "I feel guilty because I feel so hilariously happy today and explosive with joy." I may have less because I gave it away, but I gained much more in return, so much so that I don't think it was a fair trade.

We are simply stewards. Even the legacy we leave is really His legacy—since it's all His by right of creation.

THE ART OF MULTIPLYING THE TALENTS AND GIFTS YOU HAVE

—LEARNING TO MASTER
YOUR EXPONENTIAL
POTENTIAL

A nonprofit organization called a few years ago and asked if I would support its ministry financially. I believed in what the organization was doing, but I said "no."

I had a better idea.

My view has always been that giving someone a handout is never as profitable as giving someone a hand up, so I offered to pay the salary of a development director for two years who would in turn raise the funds the organization needed. The organization agreed, and by the time those two years had passed, the development director was raising five to ten times what I had been paying for his salary!

Now *that* is multiplication!

In this same vein, not long ago I paid for sixteen development people from some of the largest charities in my town to attend a special development training seminar by Christian Stewardship Association.[6] Because the mission of CSA is to influence the world for Jesus Christ by equipping Christian

> **YOU KNOW YOU HAVE MULTIPLIED YOURSELF WHEN YOU CAN'T GIVE, SEE, TREAT, SERVE, LOVE, ETC., TO THE DEGREE THAT THOSE YOU HAVE HELPED ARE NOW HELPING OTHERS!**

leaders with an understanding of biblical stewardship through education, research, resources, and networking opportunities, I knew the directors would come away with much more than an increased ability to raise financial support.

The return on my investment for sending these development directors for further training and for hiring such directors for other charities has been excellent to say the least! I could not give to every charity the amount that they are now raising for themselves. When you can't give, see, treat, serve, love, etc., to the degree that those you have helped are now helping others, *that is when you know you have multiplied yourself!*

MULTIPLY WHATEVER YOU HAVE

Every one of us has different gifts, talents, and abilities. Scripture says, "We have different gifts, according to the grace given us" (Romans 12:6). Some have more, some have less, but this does not make one person better than another. Those who boast or brag about their talents need to understand two important facts:

- ◆ First, "every good and perfect gift is from above" (James 1:17), which means our natural gifts are just that, gifts, and they are from God and are not self-generated.

- ◆ Second, "everyone who has been given much, much will be demanded" (Luke 12:48), which means God expects more from those who have been blessed with much.

Whatever it is that God has given us, whether a lot or a little, big or small, His desire is that we use it wisely so that it multiplies.

MAKING MULTIPLICATION COMMONPLACE

Though multiplication is taught in school, why is it so uncommon in real life? Here are a few reasons why:

- lack of vision
- unwillingness to let others succeed
- fear of the unknown
- selfishness and greed
- impatience
- lack of financial resources
- lack of example to follow
- insecurity
- inexperience
- lack of discipline
- pride and arrogance
- investing in something of no lasting value
- lack of knowledge
- lack of prayer
- unwillingness to change
- lack of involvement and commitment
- mismanagement
- lack of faith/belief

> GOD EXPECTS A GOOD RETURN ON HIS INVESTMENT.

As you can see, the list is primarily a list of negative attitudes, but each negative is replaceable, repairable, or changeable. *Once negatives are turned into positives, there is no reason why multiplication cannot become commonplace!*

One of the best examples of multiplication I have ever witnessed is that of the Haggai Institute.[7] The concept of the institute's founder, John Haggai, is quite simple:

1. train indigenous leaders how to reach their own people with the gospel of Jesus Christ; then

2. train these Christian leaders how to equip other people for evangelism.

Since 1969, the Haggai Institute has trained over 40,000 indigenous Christian leaders in more than 160 different nations who in turn will each train on average 100 more people. The result of the overall multiplication of the Haggai Institute has created the largest missionary force in the world, exceeding all Christian denominations combined!

Another great example of multiplication is Baylor University in Waco, Texas. In 1963 some of its leaders asked if I could help them raise more money for their college. Instead of personally going on the road or phoning all the alumni to raise the money, I took a map and had them mark where all their past students lived. Then I encouraged them to make a 16-mm movie detailing the history, present stage, successful students, possible plans for the university's future, how much money it would cost, etc. and to use these alumni as contact points.

> MULTIPLICATION IS A MINDSET BEFORE IT IS A REALITY.

They began to show this movie around the nation while recruiting fund-raising development personnel and establishing campaigns and programs to raise money.

As a result, enrollment multiplied and their $30 million

endowment has increased to over $600 million and soon will reach $1 billion, making Baylor University one of the best-endowed church-related colleges and universities in North America.

When the Haggai Institute and Baylor University overcame the obstacles that inhibited multiplication, multiplication became commonplace! It may have taken some time, but nobody would say it wasn't worth it!

BELIEF REQUIRES ACTION

If I believe in something, then I believe it ought to multiply. Belief, however, is not enough—*belief requires action if multiplication is to take place.*

For example, my grandson Brady is in a direct marketing business that is doing very well. Because I believe in the company and in my grandson, I don't hesitate to send him the names of people I meet who might be potential clients for him. It's the least I can do to support his goals, while at the same time doing what I can to help multiplication become a reality in his life.

To take action, we need to jump in. Nobody can go swimming without first getting into the water. I ask people who are trying to raise funds for an organization or charity, "Have you given to the very cause for which you are trying to raise money?" I am surprised at how many people don't even give to what it is they are trying to convince others to support! When I was selling life insurance, I bought my own life insurance, so much so that I never met anyone who had more than I did.

> IT DOES NOT MATTER WHAT WE START WITH— IT IS THE END PRODUCT THAT COUNTS.

Several years ago I met Inez Russell, an extremely dedicated woman whose passion is to help those who can't help themselves. With virtually no money and a handful of volunteers, she had founded Friends for Life to stop abuse, neglect, and exploitation through legal guardianship, money management, and independent living programs. The people she helps are unable to perform life's daily tasks, such as buying groceries, cleaning their home, managing their bills, or even changing a light bulb.

After hearing her vision and heart for those in our community, I hired a development person for Friends for Life and things quickly turned around. She now has over 2,000 volunteers to take care of 3,000 elderly people and, believe it or not, Friends for Life[8] is ranked eleventh out of thousands of charities in the United States for its overall organization and effectiveness!

A little belief and practical support in Inez Russell and multiplication was almost immediate. She had already paid the price and worked through the slow stages of planning, refining, etc. Her ministry is now being used as a template for others throughout the nation—that is multiplication on top of multiplication!

DON'T LIMIT YOURSELF

People are often restricted by what they think is reality. My house in Texas is an eighty-year-

> **NEVER LIMIT YOURSELF BY WHAT IS OR WHAT IS NOT.**

old brick house that I wanted remodeled to include an office attached to the garage. The biggest hurdle was the fact that the bricks on the face of the house were no longer in production. They were also twice the size of regular bricks and would have cost a fortune to have them specially manufactured.

Instead of giving up, I tried another option. I contacted a friend who knew someone in Mexico who worked in the brick business. With a sample brick, they gave me their estimated price—half as much as it would have cost in the U.S. for bricks half the size! Needless to say, my house and office are now the way I envisioned them to be.

By focusing on what we do not have, we limit ourselves. *We also limit ourselves by focusing on what we do have.* My incredibly enthusiastic friend Bill Armor understands this principle. He could sell saltwater to a sailor, but instead of relying solely on his enthusiasm to make a sale and build his business, he took the time to learn how to communicate, listen, and answer questions. He went on to become president of an insurance company—the fulfillment of his life-long dream. I believe he reached his goal because he didn't limit himself by what he was good at.

Multiply yourself in every way, every day, and in everything and everyone you touch. If you don't multiply yourself, something dies.

The first insurance company I worked for would not let me hire other people, so I was limited in the size of policy and the hours I could work in a single day. But the moment I was in the position with another company that allowed me to recruit other salespeople to work for me, my career took off!

My goal at one time was to recruit all the salespeople from all the other insurance companies in Florida! A pretty lofty goal, I admit, but I was able to recruit over 800 top-quality

> MULTIPLICATION TAKES TIME—*NEVER FORGET THAT!*

salespeople in twelve months! With those exponential figures in place, multiplication was a sure thing.

Also, instead of selling policies one at a time, I decided that selling to groups would be more effective. At one company I was able to sell 104 policies in three days!

Sometimes multiplication may take longer than you planned. I once heard of a university in England that was partially enclosed by a stone wall. Someone had planted an ivy bush beside the wall with hopes that the vines would grow and cover the wall, but after many years the ivy appeared dormant. Tired of waiting, the groundskeeper finally said, "Next year I'll cut it down if it doesn't grow."

The following year, to his amazement, the ivy began to

spread rapidly over the wall. Out of curiosity, he gently dug around the plant and discovered one primary root. He followed the root and found it went directly toward a river that was more than seventy feet away! For all those years, the ivy bush had been putting its entire effort into reaching the river. Once that was accomplished, multiplication took place at an alarming rate. Had the groundskeeper given up too quickly, maturity would never have been realized.

Delay is part of the multiplication process. It takes time to get everything lined up, but when that occurs, *you had better watch out because things are about to erupt!*

WHERE THE EXPONENTIAL POTENTIAL BEGINS

To multiply is to tap into your exponential potential. Though multiplication occurs in many different ways, the top six multipliers that I have experienced are:

#1 MULTIPLIER—CONNECTING TO GOD

The basis of all multiplication, I believe, begins in a personal relationship with Jesus Christ. He has an infinite amount of everything I need, far more than I could handle at any one time.

I see it like my house having the entire outflow of Hoover Dam's hydroelectric power plant at its disposal. No matter how many appliances I turn on at the same time, there is no way I will ever be able to utilize the power behind the seventeen generators inside the Hoover Dam that have the capability of supplying all the electricity needed by a city of 750,000 people! To say the least, it's far more than I could ever use or need, *no matter how hard I try!*

So it is with what God provides me. His living in me means that I am connected to the Creator of everything, including the entire solar system, the earth, and the human body. The word that adequately describes my being connected to Him is "overload," but I believe He intended that we would know our potential could never be tapped out.

By being plugged into Him, we truly have unlimited potential to grow, to increase, and to multiply. From this perspective, every limitation fades away.

#2 MULTIPLIER—BEING CREATIVE

> THE ABILITY TO BE CREATIVE IS WHERE POTENTIAL AND REALITY CONNECT.

We all have a God-given ability to be creative. However, many of us have been told so many times *what we can't do* that we have started to believe it. Instead, we need to dream and envision what we can do. *The ability to be creative is where potential and reality connect.* From there you have the ability to cause whatever you envision to come to pass.

#3 MULTIPLIER—STARTING SMALL

It is virtually impossible to get what you want by waiting for it to fall into your lap. The primary reason is that if you are not prepared to receive it, then you are most likely not prepared to keep it. Starting small is therefore a good idea.

Many years ago I invested in certain educational software to help one child. The results were so favorable that the same software was introduced to other schools, resulting in more than 5,000 schools using this educational software today. The company has also grown and is now worth millions of dollars.

> NOTHING WILL EVER GET DONE IF WE FIRST HAVE TO REMOVE ALL THE OBSTACLES.

Had I not been willing to start small, the multiplication would have never taken place. That is why Albert Einstein called compound interest the eighth wonder of the world. Something may start small, but it won't stay small for long!

#4 MULTIPLIER—LEARNING TO DELEGATE

Delegation sets the stage for multiplication, which is why I encourage everyone who works with me to delegate as much as possible. I learned this lesson of delegation many years ago from a very successful businessman and since that time have noticed a dramatic increase in my ability to dream, plan, and pursue other ideas. I only wish I had learned this lesson sooner!

#5 MULTIPLIER—ALLOWING OTHERS TO GIVE

One of the most rewarding ways to multiply myself has been to allow those who work with me to give of their time and expertise to charities *on company time.* The effect on my community has been phenomenal. Several of the local charities are among the best in the nation, not to mention the fact that thousands of lives are being positively impacted daily by our efforts.

We all need to give back to our communities. If the top executives in every town gave a portion of their time to local charities, imagine what would happen!

#6 MULTIPLIER—GIVING IT TO GOD

The act of giving up what a person wants to do is a price that most people are not willing to pay, but sadly, this is also the point where many miss the exponential growth that is intended for them. Scripture plainly states, "Unless a grain of wheat falls into the ground and dies, it remains alone; but if it dies, it produces much grain" (John 12:24 NKJV).

I've seen hundreds of boxes of fruit come from one tree that was once a very small seed. Every harvest is based on many seeds "dying," and though the seeds being planted come at a cost, the harvest makes it all worthwhile.

> **SOMETIMES DREAMS MUST DIE BEFORE THEY CAN REACH THEIR FULL POTENTIAL.**

Part of this process of dying to self includes faith that what you are "losing" will come back to you. This is where I learned what God meant when He said, "As the heavens are higher than the earth, so are my ways higher than your ways and my thoughts than your thoughts" (Isaiah 55:9).

I've turned down business deals that I wanted desperately,

simply because I felt like God didn't want me to pursue them. And later, despite my hoping, the opportunities never presented themselves again. Another time I let someone else buy the very piece of property I wanted; then a couple months later I ended up buying the same property for a better price!

Whatever happens, *I always come out better off.* That is the amazing effect of giving something to God—and letting Him multiply it.

THE FINAL GOAL OF MULTIPLICATION

When it comes right down to it, multiplication is mathematically intended to do one thing: *continue forever.*

I knew two men who were making $200,000 a year or more, but when they unexpectedly died, so did their incomes. Their wives soon found themselves in financial trouble.

This is *not* what multiplication is all about. Bringing in a lot of money, seeing a ministry grow rapidly, or watching something multiply at an exponential rate is always enjoyable, but that cannot be the ultimate goal.

In 1967, I wrote an article and then made a speech out of it. I made a tape from that speech and sold a million copies. I was paid a royalty of 25 cents apiece. Then I took that tape and the profits and made a full-length training program from the principles outlined in the tape. Over the years, millions of dollars in royalties have come from that one program!

But I didn't stop there! I took the ongoing royalties and invested them in several foundations. Today that same money is still growing and will continue to grow indefinitely, all from an article I wrote in 1967!

Through every encounter with multiplication, my goal has been to see it continue forever. *The exponential potential behind multiplication is fully expressed when growth is perpetual.*

Isn't that what a legacy is all about?

THE TRUE ROLE OF AN EMPLOYER

—BUSINESS IS ALWAYS
BETTER WHEN EMPLOYERS
KNOW THEIR ROLE

If you have ever felt "expendable" as an employee, I can relate. One company hired me to help them through a tight financial spot, then fired me when their revenue increased.

Intuitively, employers know that they would be nowhere without their employees and that sending an employee away angry might hurt business in the long run; yet every day another "expendable" employee is fired.

Why is that? It certainly isn't that there is a shortage of information on how to manage, communicate, or lead. I believe the reason is that *employers don't understand that their true role is actually that of a servant.*

SERVING IS GOOD BUSINESS

Serving employees is not as common as it should be, considering the fact that lower turnover, higher profits, greater creativity, a happier working atmosphere, and stronger unity are common results.

I focus on service in seven practical areas and the return on my investment far exceeds my expectations—*every time!* As a servant leader, I purpose to:

1. provide

2. protect

3. give respect

4. be trustworthy

5. give direction

6. provide training

7. place people over product

Employees work harder when I serve them, which makes me want to serve them even more. Then they are more committed and more willing to grow, and I want to help them more—and the cycle continues.

Perpetual motion in business is all about serving and the benefits that come as a result.

> **THE BIGGEST RETURN ON INVESTMENT COMES FROM INVESTING IN EMPLOYEES.**

#1—PROVIDE—MUCH MORE THAN MONEY.

Businesses exist to make money, but with the many components (products, services, overhead, salaries, etc.) that make the business possible, there is one part that is often overlooked: the employees.

As an employer, I have learned to take particular interest in the people who work for me. If I can help them toward their goals, they will help me toward mine—*in that order.*

In the mid-70s I asked Joe Baxter, a capable and trustworthy manager within my company, what he would do if he could do anything he wanted to do. Without hesitation he said, "I would travel the world."

At that time I needed someone to manage our growing international business, so that very day I made him a proposal that included two conditions I was sure he would like:

- You can't travel to any country without your wife; Bessie must go with you (the better his marriage, the better his long-term performance).

- You have to take time off while overseas, so work seven days if you need to but then take three days off (if he relaxes and enjoys what he does, he will perform better on the job).

He jumped at the opportunity and has since traveled to 101 different countries and set up businesses in over sixty of them! Now semi-retired, Joe recently told me, "I lived a life that only few men ever dream of, thanks to you."

Actually, the opportunity I gave Joe was really for my benefit. I saw it as an investment—the ideas he generated and businesses he established have brought in tens of millions of dollars! What he was able to accomplish was phenomenal, and as for me, the employer, *it was certainly worth the investment!*

> **"A DEAL IS ONLY A DEAL WHEN IT'S A GOOD DEAL FOR BOTH PARTIES."**
>
> —Cecil B. Day, founder of Days Inns, said this before paying a farmer twice the asking price for his property.

But for a leader who accepts the servant role, helping an employee is simply part of the job requirement. The late Cecil Day, one of the most respected businessmen of all time and the founder of Days Inns, lived by this principle. During the Arab oil embargo of the early '70s, he cut his salary to $100 a week—*and did this for a year and a half!* He did everything he could to keep the paychecks coming to what he valued the most: his employees.

Employees can be served in countless practical ways, not just because it is good business, but because it is the right thing to do.

#2—PROTECTION—FOR THEM AND FOR YOU

Several years ago, one of my employees flew to Florida for eye surgery. I was thinking about that when I realized she would have to fly back on the same airline, being exposed to germs, crowds, disruptive schedules, cramped conditions, etc. I called her in her hotel room and said, "I'm sending my Lear jet to pick you up. You'll be home in half the time."

She was so happy and relieved that she burst into tears, but in protecting her, I was doing myself a favor. She, like the others I have helped, does a better job than I ever could, which means the better I treat her and protect her, the more my companies prosper.

To the belief that "burnout is inevitable," I say that if the employer is paying careful attention to the needs of the employees, burnout is avoidable. After all, no servant would purposefully allow the person he or she is serving to be hurt in any way.

I have managers with such a strong work ethic that I have told them multiple times, "Go home! Your family is more important than what you are doing for me." However, I still find them working on weekends or late on weekdays, regardless of what I say. Aside from my concern for my employees as persons of infinite value, *I am fully aware that if they burn out, I as the employer lose the most.*

An employer who drops eighteen inches of paper on a secretary's desk just before quitting time and demands that they be completed by morning is asking for trouble. Deadlines will come, but a demanding, uncaring attitude will cause burnout quicker than anything.

> THE BEST RECRUITING DEVICE?
> **EMPLOYEES WHO ARE RESPECTED AND TREATED WELL.**

By treating employees as I would like to be treated, we all win. That is protection in its truest form.

#3—GIVE RESPECT—THEY DESERVE IT.

Without employees, we are forever limited to what we can do by ourselves, but when you add in capable and creative people, you have the potential for unlimited, exponential increase in productivity. Since that is the whole point of having employees, we must also let them know that we appreciate, need, and respect them. After all, if they are going to give their lives working for us, then we owe it to them.

Giving employees the respect they deserve will enable them to be more confident, creative, understanding, giving, and profitable. But if they don't get respect, it won't be long before they are looking for another job.

For respect to be perceived, the employer and employee must communicate or at least have a system in place that provides the necessary communication. Companies may grow to the point that a manager cannot talk face-to-face with every employee, which is fine, but respect for employees must always remain a part of an employer's temperament.

Respect that is based on the intrinsic worth of people, not solely on the kind of work employees at their level accomplish, is what enables employers and employees to connect. All employees are equally deserving of respect and should be treated accordingly.

A wise businessman once told me, "I tell every new employee, 'You do not work *for* me, but *with* me.'" His were fortunate employees.

#4—BE TRUSTWORTHY—A MUST-HAVE.

We all know of bosses and managers who promise a raise or a promotion but then never follow through with it. Raising and then crushing an employee's hopes is not only a terrible thing to do, but it completely undermines trust and long-term success.

If we are trustworthy, our employees will trust us, but to the extent that there is selfishness, stinginess, or lying in us, *they will know it!* And over time that knowledge will erode trust.

Being trustworthy and building trust also involves listening to what employees have to say. I heard of a man who had a great cost-reducing proposal.

> EMPLOYEES WANT TO BE CELEBRATED, NOT TOLERATED.

When he submitted his idea to his supervisor, he was curtly told, "We don't pay you to think; we pay you to work." Several years later the idea was finally recognized, resulting in the company saving $500,000 the first year!

Another way to build trust is to help meet employees' personal needs. If something happens at home, like a death in the family or a divorce, the employees' work is affected. To neglect these very real problems can hurt both you and your employees.

Several years ago I started using chaplains from Marketplace Ministries to help my employees with their personal concerns (as part of their benefit package). These chaplains show up on a regular basis and are simply available to talk, listen, pray and counsel confidentially.

Marketplace Ministries, founded by Gil A. Stricklin in 1984, is in more than 225 cities in 32 states with over 900 chaplains and is designed to take care of a company's most important asset: employees and their families. Increased loyalty to the company, reduction in absenteeism, increased productivity, and reduction in employee turnover are just a few of the many dividends I gain by partnering with Marketplace Ministries.[9] As an employer, it is certainly worth it to me.

Whatever is required to be trustworthy, it is worth it—and it will show on the bottom line.

#5—GIVE DIRECTION—LEADING THE WAY.

Employers must take an active role in helping their employees get where they want to go. This may even mean you lose a talented employee to another company, but if you were the employee, wouldn't you want a hand toward reaching your goals?

I had a very bright woman working in one of our companies and making approximately $25,000 a year. I saw some of the work she was doing and realized that she had talent over and above what was needed in her position. I told her she could better herself working in another profession and introduced her to a friend of mine in another company. Within ninety days she had a new job, making 75 percent more than we were paying her! She is now an independent consultant and we hire her from time to time for special projects. As her employer, directing her toward a better job was the least I could do.

But sometimes providing direction means discipline and correction, like the time I called a manager into my office who was having serious financial problems. I told him up front, "I'm not going to fire you; I want to help you solve your problems." I had him sit down with an accountant who helped him find a workable solution to what seemed to be ruining his life. He benefited, and so did I.

Employers with a servant's heart will have only good things in mind for their employees. Or, as Walt Wiley of the Fellowship of Companies for Christ International[10] says, "A servant leader leads for the primary benefit of those who follow."

#6—PROVIDE TRAINING—PREPARING FOR SUCCESS.

I take advice and training very seriously, for through it my employees get better, the company gets better, and the clients and customers are better served. As a result, if my employees need more training, I make sure they get it.

Not long ago I helped a young lady in one of our companies by paying for night classes. She graduated with her degree

> IF IT'S THE EMPLOYERS' FAULT THAT THEIR EMPLOYEES AREN'T TRAINED, THEN FIRING EVERYONE IS NOT THE ANSWER.

and now has a better job. Giving her the time, money, and opportunity was to my benefit *because a learning company is also a growing company.* Several other CPAs and MBA degrees have come as a result.

In fact, more than fifty profitable businesses in my hometown have come from individuals who once worked for me. Trying to "force" them to stay with me would have done more harm than good.

When my son Larry decided he wanted to quit working for me, I cried in my office. After ten years, he had done very well, but he wanted to launch out on his own. Today he is a successful businessman, but the letting go of such a quality individual was difficult for me, even though I knew it was for his benefit.

To foster such an atmosphere where growth, learning, and freedom are encouraged, the employer must first believe in it before it can become a reality. Some employers don't train their employees and then complain that they aren't worth their wages and deserve to be fired. But if it is the employers' fault that their employees aren't trained, then firing everyone is not the answer. Training options should always be exhausted before firing becomes a possibility.

> EMPLOYEES ARE ALWAYS MORE IMPORTANT THAN THE COMPANY, ITS ASSETS, AND ITS STOCK.

I've had many employees who seemed to plateau in the department they were working in. After speaking with them and/or their supervisor, it was easy to determine that another department would suit them better. By allowing them to move, I was gaining more satisfied employees and a more capable company.

You have to be creative with training because each person's needs are different. I once spent an entire weekend at a resort with a sales manager. He needed my help in writing an important presentation—and by helping him I was helping myself. His presentation became the most useful sales presentation our company had done to date.

In short, well-trained employees are one of an employer's greatest assets.

#7—PLACE PEOPLE OVER PRODUCT—AT ALL COSTS.

Most employers are more focused on what they do than on the people who work for them. This is a very easy trap to fall into, because without the product or service, the job wouldn't even exist.

Granted, both the product and the person are obviously necessary, but employees who feel they are less important than the work they perform will be dissatisfied and will not be the stellar employees that they could be.

By serving my employees, it is much easier to stay in touch with their personal needs, thus making it less likely that I will place my product or service ahead of them. My focus is first on them, then on what they do. This by no means lessens the importance of quality work, but it has a unique way of making the product even better.

Sometimes, placing people over a product will come at a personal cost to you. I've paid tens of thousands of dollars for employees to stay home and deal with family issues, take education classes, fly to another city for a needed vacation, and more. In addition to money, I've also spent considerable time with employees and their families, counseling, giving advice, training, or even helping them arrange financing for a home.

Not long ago, Barbara Chesser, who is one of the most dedicated employees I have ever seen, called to say that her husband had just undergone quadruple-bypass surgery and that she would come by the office later that day to catch up on her work. I had to tell her to stay home and be with her husband. "Delegate or simply tell your clients that your husband had surgery and you need a few weeks more to finish your projects," I said. "Your husband comes first; the company comes second."

Whatever the cost or sacrifice might be to you as an employer, it is worth it because of what you get in return.

APPLICATION IN BUSINESS

It is not a legal requirement for employers to apply these seven principles, but I do believe it is a moral requirement for employers who are Christians. (It is also a great way to treat customers and clients!)

I have done my best to apply these principles myself, and though I have made my fair share of mistakes, I am

> **"ANY DEFINITION OF SUCCESS MUST INCLUDE SERVICE IN IT SOMEWHERE."**
>
> —Former President George Bush

very fortunate to work with the most loyal group of people on earth. There isn't anything they wouldn't do for me—and there isn't anything I wouldn't do for them.

This mutual service, I believe, comes from a genuine love for God. That is the point where I start with my service for other people. From that, I have a strong desire to serve others, to help them, and to bless them, all because God has done this—*and so much more*—for me!

Jesus went so far as to say, "If anyone wants to be first, he must be the very last, and the servant of all" (Mark 9:35). Being an employer is all about service.

After training, teaching, encouraging, and correcting His disciples, Jesus washed their feet—a statement of humility that few today would ever make—then He went even further and died on the cross for them!

I can't top His act of service, but it stands as a stark reminder to me of how much service I can give.

PART FIVE

SETTING LIFE IN ORDER

PHILOSOPHY FOR LIVING

A financial advisor once said that people normally spend more time planning for the next summer vacation than they do making financial preparation for the future. The reason for this statistic is not that people don't care about their future, their children, or their financial well-being; *it is that they don't have a philosophy for living.*

Having a reason for what you do, whether it is financial in nature or not, is half the battle toward getting something done. Drafting your own philosophy for living will help ensure that you actually do what you want and need to do.

DISCOVERING YOUR PHILOSOPHY FOR LIVING

Everyone is different, but as for me, I am a goal-setter. This means I have a goal-awareness, a goal-setting consciousness, a goal-setting behavior, and a goal-setting habit. A long time ago I realized the only way I could be sure to achieve the goals important to me would be to plan ahead for them. Without planning, goals and purposes get pushed aside by circumstance and schedules.

At the basis of my goals lies a spiritual foundation: my relationship with Jesus Christ and my dependence on God. From that I built outward, and as I worked to clarify my thinking about my goals, using Scriptures as affirmations, I formulated a *five-point philosophy for living.*

> PEOPLE OFTEN SPEND MORE TIME PLANNING FOR THE NEXT SUMMER VACATION THAN THEY DO MAKING FINANCIAL PREPARATION FOR THE FUTURE. *IS THIS TRUE FOR YOU?*

These five points do not constitute an elaborate grid by which I measure my goals. Instead, each is a single aspect or approach to life that I hold very dear. Combined together, they form a philosophy for living that ensures I live life as I *want to* and *need to*.

My philosophy for living ties into my goal-setting nature but could just as easily be applicable to another person's temperament. Whatever it is that brings out the best in you, formulate a philosophy for living that guarantees you will get to where you hope to go.

The five points from my philosophy for living are as follows:

POINT #1—A POSITIVE ATTITUDE

I have a positive attitude and was taught that the glass is half-full, not half-empty. I've taken that principle and expanded it so that I see the glass as full, even if it isn't, and then I seek ways to make it overflow.

Someone once told me that what we are able to accomplish in life is 12½ percent education and skill and 87½ percent attitude and ability to communicate. I've come to see that this is 100 percent true, further impressing on me the belief that the power of a positive attitude is unlimited.

POINT #2—NO WORRY

I do not worry and have not for many years. Instead of worry diluting my strengths and abilities, I am filled with peace and hope. The Bible gives the best instruction and affirmation about worrying when it says, "Be anxious for nothing, but in everything in prayer and supplication, with thanksgiving, let your requests be made known to God; and the peace of God, which surpasses all understanding, will guard your hearts and minds through Christ Jesus" (Philippians 4:6–7 NKJV). Not worrying is necessary in everyone's philosophy for living.

POINT #3—PEACE AND CONTENTMENT

I have learned to be happy every day because it is a day that God has given me. And since He has given it to me, it must be good. Realistically, I know that all sunshine makes a desert, which means there will be different seasons: changes, storms, rain, growth, pruning, etc. Some days will feel great, others will feel lousy, and some will be up, while others will be down. The secret is to have peace and contentment regardless of what situation I am in, just as Philippians 4:11 NKJV says, "I have learned in whatever state I am, to be content."

POINT #4—STRENGTH AND POWER TO ACHIEVE

I see myself as an entrepreneur and a risk-taker who is courageous, bold, assertive, and willing to attempt new ideas and seek new paths. And why not? My potential to achieve is backed by the power of Christ. I know if I seek His will and make Him my constant companion and partner that He

> DRAFTING YOUR OWN PHILOSOPHY FOR LIVING WILL HELP ENSURE THAT YOU ACTUALLY DO WHAT YOU WANT AND NEED TO DO.

will give me strength and power to believe. After all, His Word boldly proclaims, "I can do all things through Christ who strengthens me" (Philippians 4:13 NKJV).

POINT #5—STEWARDSHIP

Obviously, everything belongs to God by right of creation. Out of His love for me, He has let me use some of His riches. Because I have committed my life to Christ and put Him on the throne of my life (meaning He is in control), I know that what I do is because of Him and what I achieve is because of Him.

Even the joy and pleasure I find in giving and sharing are made possible because of Him. But God, being the perfect steward, won't let us get away with acts of stewardship without blessing us more in return. He said, "Give, and it will be given to you, good measure, pressed down, shaken together, and running over will be put into your bosom. For with the same measure that you use, it will be measured back to you" (Luke 6:38 NKJV). And *that* is just what He does!

WHAT IS YOUR PHILOSOPHY FOR LIVING?

Every person should have a philosophy for living. But forming such a philosophy is not enough—*it must be written down*. I am a strong believer in writing things down because

1. writing crystallizes thought (and forces you to think out your ideas more clearly), and

2. crystallized thinking motivates positive action

Take time to write out your personal philosophy for living. It may be similar to mine, or another you've seen, or it may be entirely different. *At its core, it must express your uniqueness and reflect all the important areas of your life.*

> **WRITING DOWN A PHILOSOPHY FOR LIVING COMPELS US TO AIM FOR WHAT IS NOBLE, HONORABLE, AND RESPECTABLE.**

When you have your philosophy of living written down,

hone the words until you feel it accurately reflects your inner desires. When it is complete, print it out and place your philosophy for living in an easily accessible location. You will need to refer to it regularly until it becomes second nature for you, permeating your thoughts and actions.

After all, isn't it comforting to know where you are going and that you will eventually get there? Having a philosophy for living will not only do that for you, but it will bring far greater long- and short-term rewards than the best summer vacation ever could!

Start living your philosophy for life today!

THE IMPORTANCE OF PRIORITIES

—BECAUSE YOU LIVE
ACCORDING TO YOUR
PRIORITIES

Where you are going and what you will accomplish in life are directly influenced by your priorities. That is because the goals you set and the dreams you have are the result of your priorities. After all, of what value are goals and dreams without priorities?

Priorities are the guardrails that keep you on the road of life, especially when circumstances are difficult, people are icy, and opportunities are cloudy. All the while, priorities work to protect you, direct you, and inspire you.

When I was young and looking for a job, my dad took me to a foundry where patterns were made to produce large machinery parts out of iron. It was everything I did NOT want to be or do, and though I didn't have a well-established list of priorities at the time, I knew in my heart and mind that I could never work in a place like that. It was simply too dark, dirty, and depressing for me.

Some people take any job and try to make it work while

others complain but do nothing to change. I knew even as a young teenager that somewhere there was a career that would fit me perfectly. Until that time came, I refused to commit myself to something I knew I would dislike.

I was learning that part of having priorities is the setting of guidelines that will protect

> **TIME IS SUBSERVIENT TO YOUR PRIORITIES, BECAUSE WHAT YOU CHOOSE TO DO, YOU WILL MAKE TIME TO DO.**

me from making unwise decisions while at the same time pointing me in the right direction *and* ensuring that I get there as quickly as possible.

PRIORITIES ARE TO BE SET—THEN KEPT

Isn't it amazing that when you get a new book you've been dying to read, you suddenly find enough time to read it? The reason is that *your time is subservient to your priorities, because what you choose to do, you will make time to do.*

So it is with priorities. When you know what your priorities are—and stick to them—your day suddenly has enough time to do what is most important to you. The fact is, as Byron Weathersbee, president of Legacy Family Ministries,[11] wisely pointed out, "You don't even need to know what your priorities are—you just do them!"

Knowing what your priorities are, however, is clearly the best option. When people have poorly defined priorities, they also have a hard time saying no, even when asked to do what they already know they don't want to do. If someone asked me to do something that went against my priorities, even if it was a "good" thing, I would decline without giving it much thought.

This applies to everything, from the food I eat to the board meetings I attend. My priorities work to protect and direct me.

Here are my priorities in order of importance:

1. GOD—accomplishing His will and deepening my personal relationship with Him

2. MY WIFE—loving, protecting, nurturing, guiding, serving, and providing for her

3. MY FAMILY—loving, training, and encouraging them, and in all things, leading by example

4. MY PERSONAL HEALTH AND FITNESS—staying in shape and eating the right foods

5. BUSINESS—being a good steward with what I have and delegating to gifted, trusted, capable individuals

I consider each of these five priorities to be of utmost importance. The obvious challenge is keeping all five balanced at the same time, which is why people use the word "juggling" to describe how they manage their priorities.

> PEOPLE WHO HAVE A HARD TIME SAYING NO HAVE POORLY DEFINED PRIORITIES.

Using this analogy, the five balls I juggle would be named God, Wife, Family, Self, and Work. I have learned from experience that *not all priorities are equal.* If you drop Work, it will bounce back like a rubber ball, but if you drop any of the others, they will break or at least be seriously damaged—because they are made of glass.

When all is said and done, *priorities are only as good as they are kept.* The average husband would say his family is a priority, but how then do you explain the surveys that find fathers spend between thirty seconds and only a couple of minutes of quality time with their children each day? It is therefore no wonder that children are so highly influenced by peers rather than by their parents, especially their fathers.

The problem, people often say, is that these men have their priorities out of order. While this may be the case for some, it is my experience that their priorities are just fine—*they simply aren't keeping them.* The challenge then becomes, "How do I keep my priorities?"

HOW TO KEEP YOUR PRIORITIES

Since priorities are only good when they are kept, the "keeping" part is obviously most important. The secret is in what you do with your priorities.

For my priorities to become a reality, I must:

1. write down my priorities

2. decide that I will keep my priorities (make a commitment)

3. post my priorities in highly visible places

4. start with a very small action that daily reinforces my priorities

5. learn to do that small action right away

6. refuse to go to bed until I have done what I intended to do

7. create a visible checklist or tracking system

> MOST PEOPLE HAVE PRIORITIES—*THE PROBLEM IS THAT THEY DON'T KEEP THEM.*

8. find an accountability partner (someone I can be honest with who will be honest with me)

9. have picture reminders

10. concentrate on the benefits

11. review regularly and honestly to see if I am on target

12. choose to never make excuses

13. craft a personal mission statement (explained in more detail later)

If one of your priorities is to spend time each day with your children, then the action steps might be to set time aside so you can be together, turn off the TV, help them with their homework, work on something in the garage together, etc. By taking the opportunities that come—and not letting distractions get in your way—you will be able to keep this important priority.

> **"I'M TOO BUSY" REALLY MEANS "I DON'T THINK THIS IS A HIGH PRIORITY."**

Some of my favorite times with my children were when I was doing something (anything!) with them. Just being together thrilled my heart. Though I did spend a lot of time with my children, I wish, like most parents, I had spent more time with them.

When it comes right down to it, *priorities are habits.* And like any good habit, it takes some time for them to be established in your conscious and subconscious mind—and action naturally follows.

Your basic priorities will not change much over a lifetime, so the effort involved in making and keeping priorities is really a life-long commitment. Because of that, it is worth every effort to establish your priorities!

One of the most significant elements in making sure you keep your priorities is the creating of a personal mission statement.

WHAT IS YOUR LIFE MISSION STATEMENT?

A life mission statement serves to support your priorities. Because it runs parallel in many ways to your priorities, it works to encourage and impel you to keep your priorities.

In addition, a mission statement will also help ensure that your priorities are the right priorities. My parents told me, "Do what you do for the right reasons and keep your priorities straight." That was their way of passing their mission statement and proper priorities down to me.

People sometimes confuse a life mission statement with a philosophy for living. The difference is this:

♦ LIFE MISSION STATEMENT: your reason for doing what you want to do in life (why you will do it)

♦ PHILOSOPHY FOR LIVING: your approach to what you want to do in life (how you will do it)

Both are directly related to your priorities. Your priorities help form your life mission statement, while your philosophy for living is how you live out your priorities.

For example, my top priority is also my first mission statement and has to do with my relationship with God. Out of that relationship, which is filled with obedience to God and His Word, is one of my philosophies for living: financial stewardship with what God has entrusted to me.

> "IT TAKES DISCIPLINE AND STRONG LEADERSHIP TO SET PRIORITIES AND DO WHAT IS MOST IMPORTANT FIRST."
>
> —Hei Arita, Japan

Some might ask, "Which comes first, priorities or a mission statement?" I would say they form at the same time, and though many people state only their priorities in life, they would find—if they took the time—that their life mission statement is very similar to their priorities.

I recommend to individuals that they sit down and carefully form a life mission statement. It may, among other things, reveal something missing in their lives or even enable them to keep their previously established priorities.

A MISSION STATEMENT IN ACTION

A good friend of mine and prayer partner, Charles Williams, helped me form a life mission statement similar to his. Here is his life mission statement (used with his permission):

AS TO MY RELATIONSHIP WITH GOD

- *"But seek first the kingdom of God and His righteousness, and all these things shall be added to you" (Matthew 6:33 NKJV).*

AS TO MY RELATIONSHIP WITH MY WIFE AND FAMILY

- *Ephesians 5:23–27 (paraphrased)—I am the head of my wife, as Christ is the head of the church; therefore I will love her and give myself up for her, that she might be holy and blessed by the Word that I speak over her. We are one.*

- *Ephesians 6:4 (paraphrased)—I will love my children and grandchildren and bring them up in the discipline and instruction of the Lord.*

> **PRIORITIES ARE GOOD ONLY WHEN KEPT.**

AS TO MY MINISTRY

- *"For I determined not to know anything among you except Jesus Christ and Him crucified. I was with you in weakness, in fear, and in much trembling. And my speech and my preaching were not with persuasive words of human wisdom, but in demonstration of the Spirit and of power" (1 Corinthians 2:2–5 NKJV).*

AS TO SELF

- *Romans 12:1–3 (paraphrased)—I desire to, daily, present myself as a living sacrifice, acceptable to God, which will be accomplished by a renewing of my mind and I shall not be conformed to the world.*

- *"I have been crucified with Christ; it is no longer I who live, but Christ lives in me; and the life which I now live in the flesh I live by faith in the Son of God, who loved me and gave Himself for me" (Galatians 2:20 NKJV).*

AS TO MY RELATIONSHIP AT WORK
I desire to:

- be responsible to God and to man

- be results- and value-oriented

- be of service in an effective manner with dignity

- treat those I work for and with—and those who work for me—with love, dignity, and respect

AS TO MY RELATIONSHIP WITH THE BODY OF CHRIST
Galatians 6:1–5 (condensed):

- to teach God's Word

- to equip others in the Body

- to live and to bear one another's burdens

AS TO THE WORLD

- *Matthew 28:18–19 (paraphrased)—To live a life that will present Jesus to a sick and dying world.*

HOW TO WRITE YOUR OWN MISSION STATEMENT

Charles Williams is a reflection of his life's mission statement, so much so that if I were to describe him, I could give his mission statement and it would be both sufficient and accurate. He is one of the few people who does exactly what he says and is what he says he is.

Writing a life mission statement is quite simple. You begin by writing out your priorities in descending order, then answering the question, "What do I want to accomplish in life by keeping my priorities?" Or to put it another way, "Why do I have these priorities?"

Whether you quote Scripture like Charles did or use your

own words to answer this question, what you write should be your overall goal for doing what you do. If one of your priorities is to help people less fortunate than you, your mission statement should outline the reason for wanting to do that. If you are married and/or have children, ask yourself why you are making your spouse and/or your children a priority.

Go through each priority and thoughtfully write out the underlying reason for doing what you plan to do. This will reveal your heart or motive behind your actions. It will also further impress upon your mind why your priorities are so important. If your priorities are vague and not written down, this will crystallize your thinking and help you focus on your future.

Once you have your mission statement written down, you can keep improving on it as time goes by. By fine-tuning it, you are simultaneously fine-tuning your overall life's direction.

If priorities are the guardrails on a road, then your mission statement is the lane in which you are driving. The more closely you follow your route, the fewer corrections you will have to make and the sooner you will reach your destination.

THE BENEFITS OF A LIFE MISSION STATEMENT

Writing a mission statement is not an exercise you complete and then forget. A mission statement always inspires and directs you while at the same time protecting you from losing focus on what is most important in life.

> "YOU HIT NO HIGHER THAN YOU AIM."
> —Bob Richards, pole vault gold medallist in 1952 and 1956 Olympics

In brief, a mission statement:

1. provides inspiration, direction, focus, and consistency in all your actions

2. keeps you on track toward your goals

3. increases both your personal effectiveness and leadership because you know where you are going and your purpose for achieving your goals

4. serves as a motivator and a tool for simplifying your life and reducing your stress

5. improves your ability to evaluate your goals and make good, quick, positive decisions

Each of us tends to fulfill our own self-definitions, simply because what we say greatly affects what we actually become.

When we have carefully evaluated our priorities and mission statements and written them down, then we have a good definition from which to base our hopes, goals, and dreams.

Turning them into a reality is the next step, but with your priorities and mission statement in place, there is nothing in your way to stop you!

TURNING YOUR DREAMS INTO REALITY

—DISCOVERING THE
MAGNITUDE OF
GOAL SETTING

Goal setting is the most important aspect of all improvement and personal development plans. It is the key to all fulfillment and achievement. Confidence is important, determination is vital, certain personality traits help contribute to success, but they all come into focus in goal setting.

Probably 75 percent of my personal success has come as the result of goal setting (the other 25 percent would be a combination of focus, desire, preparation, and hard work). *I have found that if I'm not making the progress I would like to make and am capable of making, it is simply because my goals are not clearly defined.*

A goal is more than just a target toward which we move. There is something almost mystical about a crystallized goal when you have developed a plan and set a deadline for its attainment.

Such a goal produces in you a burning desire, intense self-confidence, and a firm determination to follow through. Having a wild imagination is one thing, but being very disciplined and organized will be what makes you different from the rest. *Many dream, but few dream and then fulfill.*

ANYTHING IS POSSIBLE

Goal setting is simply writing down your dreams, crystallizing your thinking, and then developing a plan with a deadline for its attainment. You can't stop a person who wants to go someplace. You can't beat somebody who won't be beaten. Setting goals will bring the right attitudes and confidence out of you, making anything possible.

In reaching your goals, you *will* face obstacles. That is a fact of life! Overcoming the obstacles, adversities, and temporary defeats will make you stronger, and that will mean when you reach your goal you will have accomplished much more than you set out

> A WRITTEN GOAL KEEPS YOU ON TRACK, SERVES AS A CHECKPOINT, AND KEEPS YOU FROM BEING OVERWHELMED BY OUTSIDE DISTRACTIONS.

to do! It is as if your achievement multiplied.

When I first started in the insurance business, I had a goal to write a million dollars' worth of business, *but I could get only one sale from fourteen presentations!* As a result, my highest monthly income during my first nine months was $87. But I believed in my goal. When I finally began to acquire the selling skills I needed, I expected to make $150 that month, but instead I made $3000.

I stuck with my goal long enough that it came together. I hit the million-dollar mark, and the second year I sold almost four million. I am thankful for every single roadblock, obstacle, and adversity I ever encountered.

If you are self-motivated and goal-directed, obstacles merely intensify your desire, multiply your energy, and make you ten times the person you would otherwise be. Foster the habit of being thankful for obstacles because all they do is push you closer to your goals.

THE #1 SECRET OF PEOPLE WHO ACCOMPLISH THEIR DREAMS

A survey taken a few years ago revealed that 3 percent of people have specific written goals and are heading directly toward them. Another 10 percent, equally as well educated and determined and do just as much thinking about their goals, the only difference is that those in the first group have *written* specific goals while those in the second group merely think about theirs. The people in the first group outperform the people in the second group anywhere from 10-to-1 to 100-to-1, which means those in the second group achieve only a fraction of the success enjoyed by the top 3 percent!

That is the power of a written goal. A written goal keeps you on track, serves as a checkpoint, and protects you from being overwhelmed by outside distractions.

The third group in the survey was comprised of more than 60 percent of the people—average people. They set their goals, for the most part, to extremely short-range objectives: the next raise, the next promotion, etc. They are just getting by financially and seldom take time to think outside of their daily routine.

The balance of those surveyed— nearly 30 percent—had never considered what they wanted out of life. They are dependent, or at least partially dependent, on others for subsistence.

> **ARE YOUR GOALS CLEARLY DEFINED?**

What differentiates those at the top from everyone else is that *the top 3 percent wrote down their goals.* Some call it a minor detail, but the difference between those at the top and the rest of society is anything but minor!

Unwritten goals are hazy goals, and a hazy goal will produce, at best, a hazy result.

THE TENDENCY OF NOT SETTING GOALS

More often than not, those who fail to set goals are the very ones who need to have goals the most. They have great potential and could go to amazing heights, but they will never fulfill their potential because they have the bad habit of not setting goals.

Noted author and radio host Larry Burkett has literally spent thousands of hours counseling people on how to manage their finances, lives, and marriages. "The lack of goal setting is approaching a crisis level," he says. "Our level of affluence [in North America] allows us to drift along in the group with relative ease and comfort. Christ said that condition would ultimately be the greatest threat to Christianity."

After years of observation, I can honestly say that Christians seem to have great difficulty with setting goals, despite the many examples and commands to prepare, plan ahead, and lead by example found in the Bible. Noah spent years building the first boat *before* mankind had even witnessed rain (Genesis 6 & 7) and he saved his family and all land animals as a result. Or consider the ant that stores its food in the summer and gathers its food at harvest (Proverbs 6:6–8).

There are numerous other examples (Nehemiah, Esther, Solomon, Jesus, etc.) that Christians would do well to consider, but none compare to God's example as the ultimate goal setter. When Adam and Eve sinned in the Garden of Eden, God's goal of restoring the relationship between Him and mankind was already set in place. It took thousands of years, but it came to pass exactly as He planned through the birth, life, death, and resurrection of Jesus Christ. If that isn't long-term goal setting, then I don't know what is!

Our goal as Christians should be "to please Him" (2 Corinthians 5:9) as we recognize and live out the reality that "the plans of the LORD stand firm forever, the purposes of his heart through all generations" (Psalms 33:11). God is into long-term growth, taking dominion, and hard work—and so should we be.

But instead of taking control, we often give up control by allowing bad habits to form. For example, I constantly hear people saying, "I don't want to take over from God—I gave God my life, so He is the One in control" or "Jesus is coming soon, so I don't bother making any long-term plans."

> "THOSE WHO ARE SUCCESS-
> FUL IN ANY FIELD ARE THE
> GOAL SETTERS. THEY HAVE A
> DESIRE TO ACHIEVE THAT IS
> COUPLED WITH DISCIPLINE."
> —Larry Burkett

To the first excuse, I would like to say, "Until you are dead, you are responsible for your own life." And if it is your responsibility, then you need to work hard and be faithful with what God has given you.

The Christian walk is exciting and full of goals, from the spiritual and the physical to the financial and the mental. If we deny this because we don't read the Bible, have been confused by others, or are just plain lazy, then it is time we take immediate action and change!

To the second excuse, I would like to remind them of the fact that a group of Christians climbed to the top of a mountain in New Zealand, vowing on national television that they weren't coming down until Christ returned. That was in 1990! Hopefully they have all returned to civilization and to their jobs and families.

Believing that Jesus will someday return is correct, but if the Bible says that we don't know the day or the hour of Christ's return (Matthew 25:13), then we ought to relax and live life like He isn't coming back in our lifetime. Then if He does, excellent! And if He doesn't, excellent! Either way we win, but when we live only for His return, we miss out on what He has in store for us now.

God has given us abilities, dreams, and far-reaching goals that will only come about by setting goals and then pursuing them now. By focusing on Jesus' return, we are missing the greatest potential of our lives here on earth—our future.

SETTING GOALS FOR YOUR SUCCESS

Each of the four different types of goals plays a part in your overall success. The first goal is the most common: *short-range goals.* These goals range from today to six months from now. Focusing on the daily actions necessary to

> WHATEVER GOALS YOU ARE SETTING— MAKE SURE THEY ARE COMPATIBLE WITH GOD'S WORD.

accomplish your goals will help you internalize the process.

The second goal follows naturally from the first: *long-range goals.* Such goals range from one year to a lifetime and express your purpose for living.

The third type of goal—*tangible goals*—are needs and wants, such as increased income, a certain trip with the family, etc. They are "tangible" because you can see and feel them, which is often helpful in the attaining of certain goals.

The fourth type of goal, though often overlooked, is the most important: *intangible goals.* These are personal goals that affect your personal character and can be spiritual, mental, emotional, etc. Usually the attainment of intangible goals (i.e., change in a certain character trait) precedes the reaching of a tangible goal. For example, when character and integrity are not properly developed, the tangible goal of owning a business or managing a larger income is usually only short-lived.

Your goal must also be something you want personally if you ever expect to achieve it. Write your goals down, no matter how silly they sound. Don't listen to inner voices that say, "I can't do that." *You can do absolutely anything you want!* And don't allow the motivational blocks in your past to limit your dreams.

After your dreams are recorded, it's time to move on to developing a plan for achieving them. Some of your dreams may be achieved quickly, others should be postponed until a more convenient time, and still others can be dropped from your list for various reasons.

MARRIED? YOU AND YOUR SPOUSE MUST ESTABLISH GOALS TOGETHER.

As you move toward your goals, use the five points I call the Paul J. Meyer Personal Success Plan, the criteria that I use to measure every goal I undertake. I do not go after anything until I ask these questions:

1. Have I crystallized my thinking about it?

2. Do I have a plan and a deadline for its attainment?

3. Do I have a burning desire? (That white heat of passion down inside myself that says I must move forward.)

4. Do I have confidence in myself and my ability to succeed?

5. Then, do I have an iron-willed determination that says I will pay whatever price necessary to get the job done, regardless of circumstance, criticism, or what other people may say, think, or do?

When you can answer "yes" to these five questions, then ask one more:

6. "Is it worth it to me?"

If you are really willing to invest the time, money, and effort required, then go after it! You have what it takes to accomplish your goal, no matter what happens, no matter who criticizes, no matter whether you have the money or not, and no matter what you now lack in experience. When you set goals without setting arbitrary limits, you are free to move as far as you want to go.

WHAT MOTIVATES YOU?

The *result* and *benefit* of your goals motivate you. People without goals are motivated by not changing, which means they only do what is comfortable for them. You often see them playing one sport, doing business one way, or treating people one way, simply because they've never done it another way and don't want to change now.

You must be willing to change. To succeed in reaching *your* goals, there are five factors to consider:

1. They must be *your* personal goals. This is a must!

2. They must be *stated positively* instead of negatively.

3. They must be *written and specific.* Dreams are general, but the plan to reach them gets more and more specific.

4. They must be *realistic, compatible, and attainable.* The day-to-day planning and walking out of your dream is what needs to be realistic. And if they fit within your value system, then they are compatible.

5. They must include *basic personality changes.* "Being" comes before "having," which means the right habits and attitudes are required BEFORE goals can be achieved.

If you have been constricted and made to fit within pre-determined boundaries, then you must prepare yourself to break out. Whoever or whatever is at fault, it does not matter. What matters is that you are liberated. Don't look back unless you want to go that way, and if you don't, then keep your gaze straight ahead.

Personally, I am confident that I will reach my goals because I practice Proverbs 3:5–6, which says, "Trust in the LORD with all your heart and lean not on your own understanding; in all your ways acknowledge him, and he will make your paths straight." Because this is both reassuring and true, I don't worry and can focus 100 percent on the tasks ahead of me.

Whatever it is you are aiming at—stick with it. Take responsibility, leave no room for the possibility of defeat, see obstacles as steps in the right direction, and keep feeding your mind with positives.

> "THERE IS NO SECURITY ON THIS EARTH; THERE IS ONLY OPPORTUNITY."
>
> —Douglas MacArthur

If I had allowed my mind to dwell on the negatives about my dismal sales performance when I was new to the insurance industry, I would have quit soon after I started. Instead, I believed I could do it, set concrete goals that I followed every single day, and before long the expected thing happened: My sales began to increase!

Goal setting takes your dreams and turns them into reality. That is the power of goal setting.

PART SIX

LIVING LIFE
TO ITS FULLEST!

FORGIVENESS! FORGIVENESS!

—SOME THINGS ARE SO
GOOD, YOU HAVE TO
SAY THEM TWICE!

Forgiveness is an incredible thing—especially when we are the ones being forgiven for wrongs we have committed. It not only feels great to receive forgiveness, but it feels just as good to forgive those who have wronged us. I say this because I know what it's like to experience both forms of forgiveness.

To me, forgiving others is like being given a reprieve from an impossible task. For a brief period of time I owned three trucks that delivered topsoil, gravel, etc. I consider carrying unforgiveness toward someone like having one of those trucks dump several thousand pounds of dirt, not on the ground, but on my shoulders!

It's an impossible weight to bear, yet we often brace ourselves and try to live with the increasing weight and pressure of unforgiveness.

What is incredible is that *we don't have to carry the load of unforgiveness!* I learned a long time ago that I could say to the truck driver, "I refuse to even have that load on my property—dump it someplace else!"

Though absolutely freeing and exhilarating, having such a mind-set does not come easily, naturally, or quickly. It takes time to develop an I-will-forgive-you-regardless-of-what-you-do-to-me mentality, but the rewards are incalculable!

FORGIVENESS HAS ITS PRICE

Those who have been hurt badly by someone and respond with, "I would die first before I forgive you!" *usually do!* There are many

> THE PRICE OF FORGIVENESS IS ALWAYS LESS THAN THE PRICE OF UNFORGIVENESS.

bitter men and women intent on taking their hurts to the grave with them. Sadly, they often die prematurely from the effects of holding resentment, anger, and unforgiveness toward another person.

We have all known people who remember a hurtful event like it was yesterday, even though it happened five, ten, or even fifty years ago. Why do they do that? Don't they know that their unforgiveness is afflicting them and everyone around them?

The reason they refuse to forgive is that forgiveness requires them to die to their "right" to be angry. Yes, they were hurt and have the right to hold that against the other person, but they also have the right to forgive and to let it go. Forgiveness has a price to pay—death to something—and that usually involves pain.

In fact, *if there were no price to pay in forgiving each other, then it would not be forgiveness at all!* But despite the heavy price that forgiveness carries with it, the price of unforgiveness is far greater! People who never forgive after fifty years have effectively been held captive for just as long—stuck in a jail they made for themselves. Their emotions, creativity, peace, joy, hope, dreams, laughter, happiness, and more have all been *minimized* by their unforgiveness.

The true price of forgiveness is just the opposite—*maximized* creativity, peace, joy, etc. Choosing to forgive or not forgive will always be our choice, but for me, it has always been one of those "no brainer" choices in life.

THE JOURNEY OF FORGIVENESS

I grew up between two polar opposites. My mom would forgive everyone and my father would forgive no one. Because parents are the best examples for learning how to forgive or not forgive, I had to choose which example I would follow.

One evening when I was young, my mother had prepared a delicious dinner, working most of the day to get it just right. When my father came home, he was in a bad mood for some unknown reason and decided to take his frustration out at dinnertime. He dumped his plate of food in his napkin and threw it out the backdoor!

> FORGIVENESS DOESN'T JUST HAPPEN. IT IS AN ACT OF THE WILL.

I couldn't believe my eyes. When I asked my mother why she didn't throw a skillet at him, she said, "I've been married to him for twenty years and have always turned the other cheek." Then she added, quoting from a Bible verse (Matthew 18:22) that meant a lot to her, "I have a long way to go until I reach 'seventy times seven.'" I could not believe my ears, but I never forgot what she said.

She could forgive because she chose to forgive. It brought her such peace and joy that it bubbled out of her life. My father, on the other hand, simply chose not to forgive, no matter how hard or awkward it made life for him or our family. I believe that his unforgiving attitudes were habits he learned as a young man in Germany, and though I don't excuse his actions, it helps me understand him a little better.

Nevertheless, what he said or did was often rash and illogical. I would be playing with a friend (the son of my father's acquaintance) one day, then the next day my dad would place my friend on a you-can't-talk-to-them-ever-again blacklist, for no apparent reason. Many friendships were broken as a result of my dad's unwillingness to forgive.

Faced with two options, I made the conscious decision to be a forgiving person, and it was a good thing too, because when I left home I experienced prejudice, injustice, scorn, jealousy, hatred, and betrayal—on a regular basis!

As I matured, the need to forgive only increased. I decided that no matter how absurd the action against me or how badly I am hurt, I will always forgive. That decision brings sanity where insanity reigns, love where there are feelings of hate, and peace where there could be war.

> "IF YOU DON'T CHANGE DIRECTIONS, YOU MIGHT END UP WHERE YOU ARE HEADED."
> —Chinese proverb

Forgiveness is a journey, one that always leads you to the same pivotal spot: the cross of Jesus Christ.

THE ULTIMATE EXAMPLE OF FORGIVENESS

At the cross, Jesus died for sins He did not commit. He chose to die, out of obedience to God, for our sins so that we could be forgiven and have our relationship with God restored.

We did nothing to deserve His forgiveness, but the necessary price for sin ("the wages of sin is death," Romans 6:23) was paid, thus making our forgiveness legitimate.

Jesus paid the price for everyone, which means our sins don't have to be held against us forever! If we confess our sins, He says He will forgive us (1 John 1:9). *That* is pretty amazing!

By rejecting Christ's offer for forgiveness, we reject the price He paid on the cross. But if we choose to accept His forgiveness, *then we also choose to forgive the actions of others toward us.* That is part of the package deal, because "if you do not forgive men their sins, your Father will not forgive your sins" (Matthew 6:15).

What this means, among other things, is that Christians should be the most joyful, peaceful, happy, loving, and forgiving people on the planet! Sadly, this is not always the case.

> **FORGIVENESS IS NOT PRETENDING SOMETHING NEVER HAPPENED.**

LEARNING HOW TO FORGIVE

Forgiveness is really for our *own* benefit, but we must be determined that we will forgive and let nothing stand in our way to do so. It is first a choice and then an action.

Sometimes a lot of forgiveness is required, sometimes only a little, but I set no limits on the forgiveness that I give to others (God did not put a limit on me!). Practically speaking, I could never figure out why people would rather have ulcers, heart attacks, emotional problems, mental problems, and more, simply because they refused to forgive those who did them wrong. I will forgive everyone, no matter what they do to me, because I refuse to settle for anything less than the benefits that come from forgiveness!

If you are having trouble forgiving, these seven steps are a good place to start:

- ◆ STEP #1—Acknowledge that you have been hurt.

- ◆ STEP #2—Recognize that your sin against God is far greater than the worst any human could do to you.

- ◆ STEP #3—Choose outright to forgive the other person(s).

- ◆ STEP #4—Accept your rightful share of the conflict, if appropriate.

- ◆ STEP #5—Try to communicate and clear the air, with hopes of restoration.

- ◆ STEP #6—Then, if nothing changes, release the person(s) and the hurt.

- ◆ STEP #7—Move on.

Throughout this entire process, I pray for the person(s) who hurt me. I want to forgive and have found it is difficult to be upset at people when I am praying for them. Restoration rests in the hands of the offending party, and though I welcome it, I leave it up to them to instigate. That is their responsibility, not mine. My responsibility is to forgive. I pray for them regularly and wish them the best, but when I move on, I don't look back.

Unforgiveness is bondage, no matter which way you slice it, but forgiveness is freedom. Some of those who have hurt me have died as a result of their actions, while others continued on with no apparent change. Whatever their case may be, I don't wish them ill, but instead focus on forgiving them and living life free from the hurt and pain that I know they are living under. Those who offend have usually been offended, and I don't want to be part of that cycle.

> **GOD FORGIVES US FOR HIS SAKE, NOT OURS!**
> "I, EVEN I, AM HE WHO BLOTS OUT YOUR TRANS- GRESSIONS, FOR MY OWN SAKE, AND REMEMBERS YOUR SINS NO MORE."
> —Isaiah 43:25

People who think forgiveness is for the weak, the coward, and the spineless have obviously never forgiven anyone. Forgiveness requires guts, determination, perseverance, courage, and love. It will test your mettle, but when your burning desire is to forgive at all costs, you will follow through.

Forgiveness is not pretending something never happened, as some have mistakenly concluded. Forgiveness is choosing to forgive *after* you have held the other person(s) accountable *and* dealt honestly with your own hurt.

If you simply write off a grievance, acting as if it never happened, then you are making God an accomplice in the wrongful action. God's desire is that you walk free and live whole, not be a doormat to be stepped on, run over, scraped up, and abused.

Through forgiveness, you can receive all the benefits He has in store for you, but it is up to you to make this happen.

If you choose not to forgive, the hurt has an uncanny way of eating away at your heart and mind. I once heard that Leonardo DeVinci, as he was working on the famous masterpiece, *The Last Supper,* painted the face of his enemy as the face for Judas. I'm sure he enjoyed the fact that he was forever immortalizing his enemy in his art, but as he did so, something strange happened—he couldn't finish the picture of Christ until he forgave his enemy. The very night he went and erased his enemy's face was the same night he finished the face of Christ. *Forgiveness unlocked his full potential.*

> **IS RESTORATION POSSIBLE? THREE STEPS TOWARD RESTORATION:**
>
> 1) *Offer opportunities for offender(s) to establish a new track record (give them a chance).*
>
> 2) *Allow time for God to work in the person's life (don't expect instant change).*
>
> 3) *Provide evaluations along the way (inspect what is expected).*

Some people don't have a problem with forgiving others—they struggle with forgiving themselves. If we first accept the forgiveness of God, then we have every right to forgive ourselves.

The results of unforgiveness affect us in a negative way, regardless of who it was (ourselves included) that did the wrong. We must choose to forgive, and then work it out, regardless!

LONG-TERM BENEFITS OF FORGIVENESS

In everything I do, I try to operate with the long-term in mind. Every house I've owned has a hedge that I planted, and though I may only enjoy it for a season, another person will enjoy it after I'm gone.

The same applies to forgiveness, except that I (and everyone I meet) can enjoy the benefits for an entire lifetime!

I must admit, the act of choosing to forgive is not easy at the moment of hurt and pain, but in the long run, it is the only way to go. The natural response may be to get mad, act hateful, and be unforgiving, but though it comes easily, *it is not the easiest route*. The easiest route is the route that brings the most benefits *in the end*, and that route is always the path of forgiveness.

Charlie "Tremendous" Jones once said, "Our unwillingness to forgive when we've been deeply hurt breeds self-pity and bitterness."

How true! But the reverse also holds true. By forgiving, we are training ourselves to be strong, confident, joyful, peaceful, happy, and loving. These positive attributes end up affecting every other part of our life.

Truly, forgiveness is amazing!

WAIT TO WORRY

—A FOOLPROOF APPROACH
TO WORRY-FREE LIVING

More damage is done by worrying than by what it is being worried about. This is because over 90 percent of all worries never come to pass.

I knew a man who was a chronic worrier; he worried about absolutely everything. For him, the habit of worrying was so ingrained in his internal system that it had become "normal." But worrying is neither normal nor necessary.

Over the years, I have made it a deliberate point not to worry. If something happens at work or at home that would constitute a worry, I have learned to address the potential worry and say, "I'm going to wait to worry." Then when I objectively and realistically address the issue, the "obvious" need for worrying goes away.

In fact, after applying my worry to the following three simple tests, *I have yet to find something truly worth worrying about!*

TEST #1—ARE ALL THE FACTS ON THE TABLE?

The most basic test usually knocks out almost every potential worry. The simple question is this: "Do I understand clearly what is being asked, needed, advised, etc.?"

> MORE DAMAGE IS DONE BY WORRYING THAN BY WHAT IS BEING WORRIED ABOUT.

If you do not have all the knowledge you need, how can you make the right decision? After you gather all the relevant data, talk with every person whose judgment on the subject you value, and read every report, *then and only then* can you act objectively and with the proper perspective.

After honestly answering this question, usually the worry dissipates and we come out the other side a better person, having increased in knowledge and overcome a difficult obstacle. The unplanned consequence of taking responsibility and answering a difficult question will usually bring a significant benefit—whether it is physically, mentally, emotionally, socially, spiritually, or financially.

TEST #2—DO I REALLY WANT TO WORRY ABOUT THIS?

For me to enjoy life, remain healthy, and be full of peace, worry cannot be part of my daily routine. What I want I must pursue, and what I don't want I must purposefully avoid.

Worrying is very high on my list of negatives I want to avoid, and it should be since I've seen its disastrous effects on the lives of people *and* their children. Here are a few of the side effects of worrying:

- ◆ SELF-DOUBT—it is a downward spiral that focuses on the negative and why things cannot be done versus why things can be done. It is a sinkhole, a debilitating attitude, and a terrible habit.

- MEDIOCRITY—capable people who worry are rendered incapable of accomplishing their intended goal. Worry makes you peck around on the ground like a chicken when you were intended to soar like an eagle.

- FRIGHT—people who worry are not being cautious or thinking things over; they are simply scared. Running scared is the enemy of success, peace, contentment, happiness, joy, laughter, etc.

- NO SPARK—the excitement is gone. Worry lets the air out of all you do, draining the fun and excitement from everything.

> "A DISTRAUGHT MIND INEVITABLY LEADS TO A DETERIORATED BODY."
> —John Edmund Haggai

- NO CREATIVITY—the freedom to be creative is squelched by worry. You simply cannot excel to your full potential when worry controls your thoughts.

- IMPROPER SHAPING—you are molded and shaped by your thinking, and worries should not shape your future.

- HAZY RESULTS—those who worry are second-guessing themselves, which produces a hesitancy that brings with it an unclear focus. Such a hazy goal will produce a hazy result.

- BAD HABITS—worrying is a habit, the result of preconditioning and years of practice. The destructive habit of worrying turns people into prisoners.

- PHYSICAL AILMENTS—the body reacts adversely to internal worries. John Haggai insightfully stated, "A distraught mind inevitably leads to a deteriorated body."

- WASTED TIME—over 90 percent of what you worry about never comes to pass. To worry is to waste time; therefore, the more you worry, the less you accomplish.

When it comes to worrying about something, the bottom line is this: "Can I really gain anything by worrying?" The answer is always a resounding "No!"

TEST #3—IS IT BIBLICALLY ACCEPTABLE TO WORRY?

This is the last and final test. If a situation can make it past this test, then it is indeed truly worth worrying about. However, the Bible plainly states many different times, "Do not worry" (Matthew 6:34). And *to do* what the Bible says *not to do* is a sin, plain and simple.

Worrying not only shows a lack of trust in God, but it flies in the face of Philippians 4:6–7 NKJV, which says, "Be anxious for nothing, but in everything by prayer and supplication, with thanksgiving, let your requests be made known to God; and the peace of God, which sur-

> "WORRY DOES NO GOOD BECAUSE IT NEVER COMES TRUE ANYWAY."
>
> —advice from an 83-year-old woman

passes all understanding, will guard your hearts and minds through Christ Jesus."

It doesn't get much plainer than that, yet people regularly choose to do the opposite of what the Bible states, then complain about the side effects of worrying. The truth of the matter is that *worry shows we don't believe the Word of God.* It is technically impossible to swim up two rivers at the same time, to sit on both sides of the fence at once, to think two thoughts at once, or to have fear and faith in the same mind at the same time.

Likewise, worry should have no place in your life. *Worry and faith are opposites.* Like cubic inches in a box, there is only a certain amount of space, so when you embrace part of one, you give up part of the other. By fully embracing trust in God and His Word, worry will naturally dissipate.

HOW TO WIN OVER WORRY

People do what they do for two reasons: to gain a benefit or to avoid a loss. But when it comes to worrying, an even more powerful force seems to take control: bad habits. They worry because it is a habit, and whether they learned it from their parents or mastered the art for themselves, the habit must be broken. The obvious question is *how*.

Entire books have been written on this subject, but I have found that regardless of the great information on this or any other topic, *people will continue to do what they choose to do*. In short, the only way to bring about change is for them to willfully choose to change their thinking.

> WORRY SETS YOU UP FOR A FALL. THOSE WHO ARE SLAVES TO WORRY WILL HAVE THEIR HOPES, HAPPINESS, AND DREAMS SMASHED THROUGHOUT THEIR ENTIRE LIVES.

The best place to start is in the Word of God. As was obvious, the third test left no room for worrying, but many people who know they shouldn't worry still worry constantly. Accepting the reality that worrying is a sin is the first step to take, and repenting (turning from it) is the second step.

Follow that with the conscious effort to fill your mind with relevant truths ("whatever is true . . . noble . . . right . . . pure . . . lovely . . . admirable—if anything is excellent or praiseworthy —think about such things," Philippians 4:8) that will equip you to withstand the habit of worrying.

And while you are reading, studying, and absorbing the principles found in God's Word, be obedient to whatever it is the Holy Spirit tells you to do. He knows you better than you do—and He wants you to be free from worrying more than you do!

Physical and mental strengthening exercises are also necessary for making the choice not to worry. I was raised not to worry. My mom said all the time to be anxious for nothing—mentally preparing me not to make worrying an option. At school not worrying meant doing my homework so that I was prepared for exams, speeches, etc., and at work it meant preparing for interviews, doing research, knowing the competition, mastering certain skills, etc.

This approach applies to all areas of life. Many people worry because they are simply not adequately prepared for what they need to do, be, or say, but I was always taught to be prepared, and that left no room for worry.

I learned to view life positively and this positive view permeates everything I do, regardless of the "weightiness" of a task. Granted, some decisions and problems are more important than others and I'm concerned about them, but being concerned is not the same as being worried.

> "IT ISN'T WORK, IT'S WORRY THAT MAKES PEOPLE TIRED AND FRUSTRATED."
>
> —J. E. Gulick

Living *with* a positive attitude and *without* worry is a great way to live. I don't expect something bad to happen, but if something bad does occur, I deal with it and get on with life. I wish with all my heart that the freedom that comes from not worrying could simply be given to another person like a letter or package, but that is not possible. Despite all the encouragement and training, it comes down to a willful choice that must be made by each individual.

We all know the facts, but people, not facts, make decisions. Make the decision for yourself to live life worry-free. It is not only possible, but it is *very* enjoyable!

LAUGHING AT LIFE

—BECAUSE ALL OF US TEND TO TAKE LIFE A LITTLE TOO SERIOUSLY

Whether you think it is good, bad, or ugly, you are experiencing life. No matter what you do, there are always things around you that are completely out of your control, like being awarded with an unexpected prize, having a tree land on your roof, or watching your stock lose half its value overnight.

Things happen that you cannot manage, manipulate, predict, or prevent. *That is life!*

However, of the things you can control, one of them has the ability to positively impact every area in your life, including the hard times. It is your ability to laugh.

FINDERS KEEPERS, LOSERS WEEPERS

> "IF YOU LOSE THE POWER TO LAUGH, YOU LOSE THE POWER TO THINK."
> —Clarence Darrow

Laughing is not a personality trait. Instead, it has everything to do with purposefully looking for things to laugh at.

Granted, there is "a time to laugh, a time to mourn" (Ecclesiastes 3:4), but people find what they are looking for.

I've trained myself to look for humor in everything that life throws at me, even in the seemingly humorless situations. I see humor at funerals, at church, at work, at home, etc. It's not that I'm out of touch with my emotions or have a warped mind, but I am purposefully looking for something to laugh at. Once the ball is rolling, it becomes much easier to see the humor in what takes place around me on a daily basis.

The French have a great adage that says, "The most completely lost of all days is that on which one has not laughed." I like that and try to make each day count.

One of my most constant sources of laughter is laughing at myself. Whoever said, "If you learn to laugh at yourself, you will always have something to laugh about," was absolutely correct. If I take myself too seriously, then I begin to think more and more about the negative situations around me. From that vantage point, discouragement, lack of faith, hopelessness, and bitterness can seep into my life.

Instead, laughter enables me to maintain a healthy perspective. A few years ago I took my long-time flying partner, Gene Franklin, out in my Piper Cub. Before we took off I asked the man who looked after my plane if it was all ready to fly, and he said it was.

> "THE MOST COMPLETELY LOST OF ALL DAYS IS THAT ON WHICH ONE HAS NOT LAUGHED."
> —French proverb

About ten minutes into the air my plane ran out of gas! I turned to Gene in the backseat and said with a smile, "What did you used to do in your car when you were running out of gas? Slosh the gas, right?"

So that's what we did. I turned the plane around and headed back, sloshing the tanks whenever the engine started to sputter. We made it to one airfield and were about to land when I remembered there was no gas there, so I said with a laugh,

"Perhaps we can make it three more miles."

By now we were well past empty, but by sloshing the tanks from side to side we made it those three miles. As we were coming in to land, the engine finally quit, as did the propeller. We coasted right up to the gas tanks and ran out of momentum just three feet away! As the gas attendant fueled my plane, he remarked, "I didn't know these little planes held so much gas!" We had a good laugh at his comment.

The situation was serious and could have been disastrous, but worrying or stressing myself out would have done nothing to make the situation any better. In fact, doing so would probably have made it worse by impairing my ability to think clearly. I laughed at myself for not checking the fuel gauge (it's always the pilot's responsibility to do so) and it is a lesson I know I will never forget!

Gene even laughed, and though I would have *never* flown again with a pilot who forgot to check his own gas, he has flown with me many times since then. In addition to being a good flying partner, he is a good laughing partner—something that each of us needs to find in life.

WHY NOT LAUGH?

There is always a reason to laugh. Sure, there is probably also a reason not to laugh, but you have to choose which one you want to do. Here are five reasons why cultivating the habit of daily laughter is beneficial:

#1—LAUGHTER IS BETTER THAN TEARS.

My mother could laugh at anything. It was not that her life was perfect, but rather that she chose laughter instead of sadness, resentment, or discouragement. Every coin has two sides, and so does every situation.

She would find the best side and focus on that, and at times, she would find humor or insight in something that would have thrown another person for a loop. Many times she told me to see the other side in something that was cruelly said or done, and when I did, the hurt or anger would disappear. She helped train me to laugh and to find humor in life.

Since there are always two choices, choose laughter every time.

#2—LAUGHTER IS GOOD FOR YOU.

Laughing isn't just a good option or the lesser of two evils; it is actually good for your health, just as Proverbs 17:22 says, "A cheerful heart does good like medicine, but a broken spirit makes one sick" (TLB).

Numerous studies, articles, books, and speeches have detailed the fact that people have used laughter to recover

> IF YOU LAUGH AT YOURSELF, YOU'LL ALWAYS HAVE SOMETHING TO LAUGH AT.

from serious illnesses. Sadly, the power in laughter is only intermittently tapped into.

Laughter has been shown to lower blood pressure and boost the immune system, but does that translate into a longer life? I read about a university that tested this theory by asking a group of men and women (average age, seventy-two) to compare their sense of humor to that of a sibling who had died (at the age of sixty-five, on average). Sure enough, most said they laughed more than their sibling ever had, suggesting that he or she who laughs, lasts.

People take money very seriously, and to some degree that is only appropriate, but even money is not so important that you can't laugh at its gain or loss. I've awakened on Monday mornings to find that some of my stock investments have dropped sharply or increased dramatically.

Of course I prefer the increases, but the losses make me shrug my shoulders and say, "You win some, you lose some, and some you get rained out." The gains make me laugh and say, "I'd be dangerous if I knew what I was doing."

We stress out over things in life that are not really all that important, so much so that stress has become the greatest single contributor to illness in the industrialized world. People are beginning to discover just how interrelated the mind and body really are. Laughter is good for you!

#3—LAUGHTER IS POWERFUL.

Those who know how to use humor effectively are usually the ones who know how to persuade others. The ability to make others laugh and to employ humor as a tool in defusing potentially troublesome or awkward situations is a valuable human resource. Best-selling author and famous motivational speaker Zig Ziglar uses this approach with his audiences and even tells them, "It's hard to be upset at someone when you're laughing at him."

It's true! If people are laughing at you, you can tell them almost anything, but if they are upset at you, even a nice "pleased to meet you" may set them off. Humor is an attitude that can be learned and practiced. Once learned, this attitude can make a meaningful difference in your self-concept, in setting and approaching goals, and in handling interpersonal relationships.

Laughing also has the power to change your own world, to make you see things in their proper perspective, and to enable you to keep going, even when opposition seems insurmountable.

> "IT IS GOD'S WILL, NOT MERELY THAT WE SHOULD BE HAPPY, BUT THAT WE SHOULD MAKE OURSELVES HAPPY."
>
> —Immanuel Kant

When I was young and in full-time sales, I used to smile and say to myself, "Everybody can be sold by somebody . . . why not me?" Instead of taking life so seriously, I used laughter to help motivate me to achieve my potential. I once met a prospective client *wearing* my product—chocolate drink—all over my business suit! I had slipped coming down a flight of stairs, spilling the contents of the portable drink machine all over myself. Although I didn't make the sale, we both had a good laugh.

If laughter has the power to move you, inspire you, and heal you, then it has the power to change those around you as well.

#4—LAUGHTER IS FUN TO BE AROUND.

Humor gets people's attention and brings them together. Besides being a must for public speaking—since the goal is to keep their attention—it is simply fun to be around people who laugh a lot. They are upbeat and positive, rather than discouraging and judgmental.

Bill Hinson, a friend I've had since I was twenty years old, is a master of humor. I've seen him use humor to calm arguments, to explain a delicate situation, and to make someone feel comfortable.

With his humor and laughter, it is no wonder to me why he held so many positions of leadership throughout his life. When Bill walks in the room, everyone knows it. His phone calls are always encouraging and his presence lifts your spirits. When he is around, you know it. He is a blessing.

Solomon, considered to be one of the wisest men of all time, said, "Two are better than one," then added, "for if they fall, the one will lift up his fellow" (Ecclesiastes 4:9–10, KJV). I think that applies to laughter in that when one is down, the other is able to lift him up through the strength and power of laughter.

Laughter brightens our good times and lightens our heavy times. Since we go through life with other people around us, we might as well enjoy the ride. Laughter is the life of a party, and if others don't want it, we should take their share as well.

Proverbs 17:15 says that the "cheerful heart has a continual feast." Well, I've found from experience that where there is food, people will congregate. And if it's a continual feast, then you are sure to have a crowd. Why not be the one who hosts the party?

#5—LAUGHTER IS A GOOD TEACHER.

Laughter is one of the best teachers of all time. If you are responsible for training people, especially children, then laughter ought to be used to your advantage.

I heard of a father who used humor to teach his daughter a valuable lesson. She had excessively overpacked for a short stay with her cousin. Instead of lecturing her, he put on the most pitiful look he could, to which she asked, "What's wrong, Daddy?"

He replied, "I thought you were going for a couple of days. I didn't know you were moving out!" She laughed, and agreed.

If you have traveled overseas, you have no doubt discovered the different customs each country has. Breaking these culturally taboo rules can be some of the most embarrassing, yet humorous, experiences. Teaching these customs using humor is natural, yet it both diffuses the potential ill will toward the foreigner and enables the foreigner to never forget his or her blunder.

Whatever it is you do, include laughter and you will see the results improve.

LAUGHING ALL THE WAY HOME

Someone asked my wife, Jane, what she liked most about me. She instantly said, "He makes me laugh." I had never heard her say that before, but of course it made me feel good.

Marriage is a great place to foster a lifelong attitude of laughter. Whether you are married or not, it would do you well to heed the following advice from author Dr. Barbara Chesser. I've known Dr. Chesser for years and can vouch for what she says—because it works!

We know that a sense of humor helps put things into perspective, but sometimes it doesn't come so easy. Without laughter, molehills can become mountains and every flaw in our marriage partner can stand out like a sore thumb. A marriage ought to be fun, and it can be, if laughter is cultivated.

Here are Dr. Chesser's tips for making laughter an integral part of your marriage:

+ Learn to lighten up, live a little, and laugh a lot.

+ Be sensitive to differences in sense of humor, especially if you and your spouse vary in this area.

+ Consider the timing of your humor.

+ Don't laugh *at* someone; laugh *with* them.

+ Establish your own ground rules.

Then laugh when:

+ there is nothing you can do but laugh

+ one or both of you do not understand what to do next

+ one of you has an overriding urge to kill the other

+ you need to preset your mind to handle in a positive way a potentially negative situation

+ you need a safety valve to help heal the hurts of grief

> **"FORTUNE COMES TO THOSE WHO SMILE."**
> —Japanese proverb

Laughter is more than good medicine—it is the *best* medicine! Whatever you do, learn to laugh at life.

You owe it to yourself and everyone around you not to take life so seriously!

PART SEVEN

THE GREATEST
LEGACY OF ALL

THE GREATEST LEGACY OF ALL— KNOWING GOD

—FROM THIS, EVERY OTHER LEGACY GAINS MEANING AND PURPOSE

When I was a boy, we were never financially well off. However, during World War II, what we did have we sent to some of our relatives who were trying to survive in war-torn Europe. My dad had me help him box up small cartons of dried fruit, jams, nuts, etc., and we would mail them to his relatives. Every few weeks we would send out another package, yet we never heard if they were arriving.

Perhaps the food ended up on the table of an enemy soldier or in the hands of a hungry mailman. We never knew, but my dad thought it was important, so I helped him.

THE ELEMENT OF TRUST

Over fifty years later, after tracking down some of my parents' ancestors in France and Germany, I found myself at the home of my dad's relatives, the very family we had mailed the packages to so many years before. As we chatted, the discussion turned to World War II, and out of curiosity I asked my cousin if they ever received any of the boxes my father and I had sent.

He paused, and when he looked at me I noticed his eyes were brimming with tears. His voice cracked as he said, "We survived because of what you mailed to us. We would not have made it otherwise."

> "GOD WANTS US TO KNOW HIM DEEPLY BECAUSE HE KNOWS WHAT KNOWING HIM WILL DO FOR US."
> —Peter V. Deison

All those years and I never knew! All the work and effort was instantly worth it as he gave me a hug that was filled with such warmth and gratitude that I too began to weep.

My level of trust for my dad went up several notches that day. If he were still alive and wanted me to send a care package to someone, I wouldn't hesitate. Why? Because I knew him well enough to trust him completely.

In the same way, the more we know God, the more we will trust Him. It is a process that takes time with markers along the way that indicate our progress.

MARKER #1—TRUSTING GOD

The trust I had for my dad came from knowing him and from experiences with him. In a relationship with God, no two people are alike, which simply means that none of us will experience God in the exact same way (experience is not the only way to know God, but it can certainly work).

Author of *Knowing God*, J. I. Packer, says that God takes people (i.e., Jacob, Joseph, and others) to the bottom of life so that they can live at the top. Why does God do this to us? Because He has great things in store for us and He desires to get us where we need to be—*and that always includes trusting Him.*

Whether taking people to the absolute bottom so they can live at the top is mandatory or not, I cannot say. I do know, however, that I've been to the bottom several times myself *and it was worth it every time!* What I gained in my knowledge and trust of God was of such value that I would not trade it for the world.

No, it wasn't a piece of cake, but it sure was good for me. The bottom line is that God wants me to trust Him. Though He will never force me, He will go to great lengths for me to trust Him—and He does this for everyone!

> "I THANK GOD TODAY FOR THE HARD, HARSH, ABRASIVE TIMES THAT RAKED MY EMOTIONS AND ABSOLUTELY PULLED OUT FROM UNDER ME THE THING THAT I WAS HANGING ON TO . . . SO THAT THERE WAS NOTHING LEFT BUT GOD."
>
> —Chuck Swindoll

Experiencing God authors Henry T. Blackaby and Claude V. King explain that God uses us for something "big" when we are truly ready. The getting ready part must always come first, for through it we trust and know God.

Abraham is one of my favorite men in the Bible. Though he made plenty of mistakes, he never quit. He doggedly desired to know God and to obey Him. When God told him to sacrifice his son Isaac (Genesis 22:2, 13), he obeyed. At the last second, an angel showed him a ram caught in a thicket and he sacrificed the ram instead. Through his obedience he discovered more of God's character and called God by a new name, *"The-Lord-Will-Provide."*

Like Abraham, I have seen God provide many times and my faith and trust toward God has grown every time. Also like Abraham, sometimes I don't always see the end result of my actions, but I obey in faith. For instance, I've felt I should help certain people financially, only to find out later that they were taking advantage of me. Didn't God know that? Didn't He see what was happening? Of course He did, *but my job is to be obedient, not to know all the answers.* Through my obedience, however, I know God better, which is probably the whole point.

God proved Himself to Abraham and He has proven Himself to me—He is *completely* faithful, true, and trustworthy. And He will prove Himself to you!

When all was said and done, Abraham knew God on a personal level. He understood His character and found Him to be who He claimed to be. In fact, Abraham went on to be called a friend of God (2 Chronicles 20:7). Now *that* is a legacy!

WHERE TRUST WILL LEAD YOU

To trust God will require two very separate willful choices that nobody else can make for you. Parents *can* and *should* lead their children up to the door of each decision, but as it is with any legacy, the final answer will always rest with the child.

The first decision is the most important one:

> **WE OFTEN DON'T TRUST GOD, YET HE IS**
> —*never late*
> —*never unfaithful*
> —*never cruel*
> —*never absent*
> —*never unloving*
> —*never wrong*

#1—DO YOU TRUST GOD WITH YOUR ETERNITY?

When I was 16 years old and standing alone in a grape vineyard, I made that decision. Jesus said, "I am the door: by me if any man enter in, he shall be saved" (John 10:9 KJV), and my mother led me to that door. I made the willful choice to confess my sins and ask Jesus into my heart—and I stepped through the door.

Like any relationship, it takes time to get to know the other person. The more I learned of God's character and His love for me, the more I trusted Him. The next decision followed:

#2—DO YOU TRUST GOD WITH YOUR DAILY LIFE?

Eternity is forever, while a mere seventy to ninety years on earth in comparison is nothing more than one small drop in an ocean-size bucket. Why are we quick to trust God with our eternity, yet we struggle with trusting Him in our daily lives?

This decision for many people is the most difficult because it is where they start dealing with very practical and personal issues, such as attitudes, desires, thoughts, emotions, and money. I believe with all my heart that God simply wants us to trust Him.

What would cause a person not to trust God since He is never late, never unfaithful, never cruel, never absent, never unloving, and never wrong? *Is it because we have been preconditioned to believe otherwise?*

If you—like me—have had plenty of trust-defeating experiences, don't hold that against God. The fact is we can trust God because He is "perfect, and all his ways are just. A faithful God who does no wrong, upright and just is he" (Deuteronomy 32:4).

Regardless of what might happen or what anyone might say, perfect is perfect. And in addition, He desires that we experience "life, and life more abundantly" (John 10:10).

God is trustworthy, perfect, and on your side—how can you not love Him?

MARKER #2—LOVING GOD

God doesn't only offer select people the opportunity to know Him. Instead, He wants to have a personal relationship with everyone, but He will never impose on us.

I've tried to *make* certain people be my friends and found out quickly that it doesn't work. It has to be a mutual desire by both individuals. But with God, He is already waiting for us.

Is it possible to know God as you know your best friend? I believe the answer is yes, though you obviously cannot sit down with God and have a cup of coffee together. The relationship is different, yet it's the same—even better!

Going for a walk with my wife is *the method* by which I get to know her. What we do is not as important as the fact that we are together and that I am listening to her, seeing her for who she is, and seeking to understand her.

Christians have sought to know God for generations yet have struggled with questions like: "How many chapters do I need to read in the Bible . . . How long should I pray . . . What happens if I miss one day . . . Is ten minutes long enough?"

Such questions are missing the point. *They are focusing on the* method *instead of the* reason *for getting together in the first place.* This improper focus on method is legalistic and, as is expected, will stifle any relationship.

I spend time with Jane because I love her, not because I am ordered

> "SEEK TO KNOW GOD BY REVELATION, NOT BY EXPERIENCE OR EDUCATION. IF IT IS BASED ON EXPERIENCE OR EDUCATION ALONE, THEN THE YOUNG CAN'T KNOW GOD AND THE OLD SHOULD KNOW HIM THE MOST—AND NEITHER OF WHICH IS TRUE."
>
> —F. Nolan Ball, pastor, age 73

to. In relation to God, our love for Him is not limited to something we feel good about, like an emotional high from a certain experience. Instead, Jesus commanded, "Love the Lord your God with all your heart and with all your soul and with all your mind" (Matthew 22:37).

Quite simply, we are to love Him with everything we are, wholly and completely. And the more you love Him, the more you know Him—and the more you know Him, the more you love.

MARKER #3—OBEYING GOD

Obedience is the natural next step in a relationship with God, but you admittedly have to know what He is saying before you can obey Him. Hearing His voice is therefore a vital part of knowing God, as no relationship ever consists of one-sided communication.

God seldom speaks audibly, though He does speak constantly through His Word and His Holy Spirit. (He also speaks through other people, circumstances, and more—and everything He says is in line with His character and His Word.)

When I made Him Lord of my life, I gave up the right to say no to His commands, so when He speaks, I am to obey. That is where the growth, breakthrough, and blessing take place.

Many years ago I had an especially pivotal breakthrough in my knowledge of God. The circumstances were neither comfortable nor particularly enjoyable, but the transforming of my knowledge *about* God into knowledge *of* God was meaningful and lasting.

> "WHAT A MAN TRULY KNOWS, HE WILL LOVE, AND WHAT HE TRULY LOVES, HE WILL SERVE."
> —Dr. Dwight Pentecost

I had invested a lot of time, energy, and money into a business venture that was ready to be launched to great heights. However, at that point I found myself in a difficult situation: proceed against my morals and business ethics based on God's Word or let the business die at the starting gate. I chose the second option.

Within days I was offered an opportunity that eventually led me to where I am today. Had my business venture been a success, only God knows what my life would be like today.

Through that experience, I came to understand that God was a whole lot more interested in my welfare than even I was! By obeying Him, I benefited in every way possible.

MARKER #4—SERVING GOD

In our progressive relationship of knowing God, there is an important reason for listing "Serving God" as the *last* marker. People who place it first often accomplish great things for God, though many times they fail to have a personal relationship with Him along the way.

Scripture plainly states, "And this is eternal life, that they may know You, the only true God, and Jesus Christ whom You have sent" (John 17:3 NKJV). Since knowing God is eternal life, then it only makes sense that our focus be on knowing God rather than on serving Him.

This by no means minimizes the importance of what we do for God. Usually, we end up serving as we obey Him. In fact, Ephesians 2:10 reveals that God prepared good works "in advance for us to do"! God cares greatly about what we do for Him, and so should we.

Some of the most meaningful and enjoyable times I have ever experienced in life have come as I served other people out of obedience to God.

- I've given my coat to someone who needed it more than I did—I was so warmed on the inside, I could have stayed outside in the cold weather all day!

- I've helped hundreds of young people go to college—I am incredibly excited about their futures and love being able to play a part of it!

- I've helped take care of my employees in many ways—I am fortunate to help them and always end up being blessed more in return!

- I've given to organizations that help the homeless, the rejected, the hungry, and the lost—and I am humbled yet invigorated as I help!

> "IT IS EASY TO KNOW A LOT ABOUT GOD WHILE NOT KNOWING MUCH OF GOD. WE CAN EVEN BE GOOD WITHOUT KNOWING GOD."
>
> —J. I. Packer

The happiness that comes through service that originated in obedience is so intense that words can't adequately describe it! *You will have to experience it for yourself!*

KNOWING GOD'S HEART

Peter V. Deison, in his book *The Priority of Knowing God,* wrote, "God wants us to know Him deeply because He knows what knowing Him will do for us."

That is precisely God's heart. He gives back to us far more than we could ever give to Him. He loves to bless us, give to us, and be with us simply because He is our Father. As a father myself, I know what it is like to want to bless my children and grandchildren—*only God desires to do that for you in a multiplied fashion!*

Knowing God is the greatest legacy of all!

WALKING WITH CHRIST

—THE LIFELONG JOURNEY THAT NEVER ENDS

Looking back to the day I asked Jesus into my heart, I had no idea how it would impact my life (I don't think anybody really knows until later). I did recognize, however, that following God would be a journey.

"Is it hard to follow God?" people have asked me. It depends on your definition of "hard." Does following God come with a cost? *Absolutely!* Are there wants and desires along the way that you give up? *All the time!* But is it hard to follow Him? The answer is a resounding *"No!"*

Cost and self-sacrifice do not make something hard. Nobody feels sorry for the athlete who wins an Olympic medal, even though that person paid an incredible price through grueling effort behind the scenes, denying himself or herself certain things, probably for several years, all for one hopeful brief moment of glory. The medal, once attained, minimizes every cost and self-sacrifice.

Following God is similar in many respects. There are costs

and self-sacrifices to be made, but that does not mean it is hard to follow God. Hard is when you compete but never win, invest but lose everything, work but receive nothing for your efforts, and show love but receive hate in return. *That* would be a hard life, but that is not the life I have lived!

When I compare my costs and self-sacrifices with what I have already received and will receive in return, my costs and self-sacrifices are insignificant!

> COST AND SELF-SACRIFICE DO NOT MAKE SOMETHING HARD.

WHAT DOES IT MEAN TO FOLLOW GOD?

I saw following God as my role as a Christian. After all, I am the sheep and He is the Shepherd, I am the servant and He is the Master, and I am the creation and He is the Creator. In every paradigm, I am the follower and He is the leader.

It is correct that God is all these things (Shepherd, Master, Creator), but He is so much more! Scripture also says that He is:

+ my father (Romans 8:15)

+ my brother (Hebrews 2:11)

+ my intercessor (Romans 8:34)

+ the atoning sacrifice for my sins (1 John 2:2)

And I am:

+ a child of God (Romans 8:16)

+ a new creation (2 Corinthians 5:17)

+ a joint heir with Christ (Romans 8:17)

As I began to see that Christ was my Lord and Savior *and* my brother, intercessor, father, and even friend, my perception of Christ and my relationship to Him changed dramatically! Now it was possible to actually walk *together!*

It is cultural in some countries for a husband and wife who are walking together to actually be several paces apart—the husband in front and the wife behind. This same image is how I envisioned myself walking with God.

Jesus did initially greet His future disciples with, "Come, follow Me," but He didn't tell them the same thing every day because they were already *with* Him. Scripture says that "He [Jesus] lives in us" (1 John 3:24 NLT). Because He is already in me, I don't need to chase after Him—we are inseparably linked. He even says, "Never will I leave you; never will I forsake you" (Hebrews 13:5).

> THE JOURNEY OF A CHRISTIAN IS ONE THAT REQUIRES A TICKET HE CANNOT AFFORD, GOING TO A DESTINATION HE DOES NOT DESERVE.

Clearly, God wants more of a relationship with me than a slave has with his master or a king with his subjects. I find it amazing that God would allow me, a man who grew up as a fruit picker in California who at times had a foul mouth and who never earned a college degree, to inherit *everything* that He has for me! Why would God give me what I do not deserve and could never earn?

There is one word to describe it: grace.

THE JOURNEY OF GRACE

Grace is a word that people use but seldom understand. Grace cannot be confused with mercy, for mercy is letting you off the hook for something you did or rightly deserve. Instead, grace is giving you something you do not deserve *and* could not get, buy, gain, or earn, no matter how hard you try. Steve McVey, author of *Grace Land*, put it another way: "Grace means that God does it all."

God has given me so much, all of which I do not deserve, no matter how morally upright I might try to be. Scripture says, "For all have sinned and fall short of the glory of God" (Romans 3:23). Death should be my lot in life as a sinner, but God has given me life. He then adds to it so that my life overflows with His goodness, kindness, and generosity. God does nothing halfway! He said, "I have come that they may have life, *and have it to the full*" (John 10:10, emphasis mine).

> GRACE IS GOD GIVING YOU SOMETHING YOU DO NOT DESERVE *AND* COULD NOT GET, BUY, GAIN, OR EARN, NO MATTER HOW HARD YOU TRY.

But Jesus does not stop there. He took my image of me following Him like a dutiful sheep and turned it upside down when He said, "I am the good shepherd. The good shepherd lays down his life for the sheep" (John 10:11).

He gives me what I don't deserve, He desires to bless me beyond what I can handle, and then He dies for me! What type of one-sided relationship is that?

Along the journey with Christ, there are countless detours that promise a better way, an easier way, or a smoother way. However, *no detour off God's path will take us back to His path.* Scripture says that narrow is the road "that leads to life, and only a few find it" (Matthew 7:14). Once we find it, there is no reason to get off, regardless of the seemingly insurmountable obstacles in our path or the appeal of the detour.

I have encountered many detours myself, including the following three:

1. the path of least resistance

2. saved by grace, living by works

3. wanting to be like Christ

These three detours are also reoccurring, catching people off guard when they least expect it. Thankfully, God thought ahead by providing the Holy Spirit to keep us aware of our location and by allowing us to get back on track through repentance and forgiveness.

DETOUR #1—THE PATH OF LEAST RESISTANCE

If I choose *not* to obey God and instead do what I want to do, I have just taken the path of least resistance. This detour becomes a viable alternate route when I begin to think, "I'm tired of giving up my wants and dreams. What I want is most important."

God doesn't ask us to give up everything in life, but there are certain times when His plans and our plans don't match. When we die to our own agenda and obey what He says to do or not to do, we stay on course. The truth of the matter is that when I disobey and do what I want, it ends up hurting me more

> RESISTANCE ALONG GOD'S PATH IS DESIGNED TO MATURE ME; RESISTANCE ON A DETOUR IS DESIGNED TO DESTROY ME.

in the long run than if I had obeyed God in the first place.

This giving up of our own desires in obedience to God (dying to self) does not guarantee smooth sailing. There will still be bumps in the road, but *resistance along God's path is designed to mature me, while resistance on a detour is there to destroy me.*

When I was young, I did not understand that dying to self is simply the first part of the overall process of preparation; the second part is God rebuilding me. Over and over this process continues, just like a potter with a piece of clay. Isaiah 64:8 says, "We are the clay, you [God] are the potter." The reason for this repetitive rebuilding is so that I become pure, clean, and whole, which is only possible when He removes my selfishness out of the equation.

Taking the path of least resistance is not always a defiant act of rebellion or the result of chasing after something bad. I may want to accomplish God's will, but when I try to do it in my own strength, I am taking the path of least resistance and on a detour nonetheless. God wants to do it His way through me—the talent, ability, drive, determination, and discipline that I have are not the answer.

The more I understand the process of preparation, the more I allow my selfish ambitions to die. As a result, I have willingly traded:

- my wants for His wants

- my "big" dreams for His dreams

- my plans for His plans

- my goals for His goals

- my abilities for His abilities

- my gifts for His gifts

- my hopes for His hopes

- my life for His life

> "THE COURSE OF LEAST RESISTANCE MAKES CROOKED RIVERS AND CROOKED MEN."
> —William Danforth

In each of these cases, I've come out far better off than before! God is a giver and not a taker; He always reciprocates to a larger degree.

When I let Him work through me, something remarkable takes place. Romans 8:19 says, "The creation waits in eager expectation for the sons of God to be revealed." I became a son of God at salvation, but I am not "revealed" until I have learned to die to myself. At this point, He is free to use me in any way He wishes and the path of least resistance is revealed for what it is—nothing more than a dead-end road.

DETOUR #2—SAVED BY GRACE, LIVING BY WORKS

Scripture says, "It is by grace you have been saved" (Ephesians 2:5). Nobody deserves salvation and there is not a single person who could work his or her way to heaven. Nonetheless, good works have been mankind's "best shot" at salvation for thousands of years.

When people find salvation in Jesus Christ, which they recognize is a result of grace, they often turn around and begin to rely on their good works as a basis for their right standing with God. Christians would not likely admit this, but it's true! I know because I have been down this detour many times myself. When I realized the truth, I quickly repented and got back on the right road.

The fact of the matter is that I cannot live the perfect Christian life. I will make mistakes. I'll never be good enough or do enough good deeds to please God—*it is not possible to do so!* Reliance on good works is nothing more than a detour that actually separates me from my relationship with Christ.

God is perfect and He demands perfection, which means I would lose every time. But when I surrender my life to Jesus, God accepts

> DENYING SELF TREATS THE SYMPTOMS, DYING TO SELF SOLVES THE PROBLEM.

me. I must relax in the fact that I cannot improve on my current condition. Sure, what I do is important, but my righteousness does not come by what I do; it results from *who I am* as a believer in Christ.

For me, I am continuing to understand more and more about the grace that God so freely gives. Because of grace:

- God expects nothing in return for what He has done for me.

- God will never give up on me.

- God sees me as righteous.

- God doesn't want me to lead others to morality, but to Christ.

Is it possible to take grace too far and begin to do my own thing, living a life that is an embarrassment to Christ? Not if I truly love God, because if I love God, I will do what pleases Him. In essence, I am free to do whatever I want since what I want is what God wants.

Am I weak because I recognize that I cannot do things in my own strength? No, I am strong, because, as God Himself says, "My grace is sufficient for you, for my power is made perfect in weakness" (2 Corinthians 12:9). People who believe otherwise are hoping that good works will do something for them that they never did for anyone else.

Accepting and applying the fact that God uses my weaknesses has been difficult for me. I had a German father who told me on more than one occasion, "God gave you a brain, use it!" The obvious subconscious message was to become self-sufficient. As I have grown in my Christian walk, I've had to think through that subconscious message and reverse it.

My mother also said, "You have right here between your ears everything you will ever need to succeed." The message was that I was the fertile ground—I just needed to plant the right seeds. Again, the implication was that I could exercise my initiative to make things happen, which to some degree is correct, but an unbalanced view can do more damage than good.

In fairness to my parents, they came from different countries, from a different time, and with different circumstances. Nonetheless, certain things they taught me were an obstacle to my Christian walk.

Today I recognize that it is simply impossible for me to live the Christian life in my own strength. Struggling to live a godly life is a painful detour that takes me further and further away from the joy and freedom that Christ intended. I need to trust Jesus Christ to be Himself *in* and *through* me.

That not only takes pressure off of me, but it excites me to see how God uses me. I've prayed for years that God would allow me to influence other people every day for Him, and sometimes I'm amazed at the results.

> "RELIGION OFFERS THE FALSE HOPE THAT SOMEHOW THERE IS SOMETHING WE CAN DO TO IMPRESS GOD ENOUGH TO CAUSE HIM TO ACCEPT US ON THE BASIS OF OUR ACTIONS."
> —Steve McVey, *Grace Land*

I once woke up in the middle of the night and wrote a note to a woman who was trying to attend college. I enclosed a check and mailed it the next afternoon. A few weeks later I received a letter from her saying how the money came at the exact moment when she needed it the most. How could I have known? Was it me or was it Christ through me?

Another time I spoke with a man and said something that changed his life dramatically as a result. Was it me or was it Christ through me?

Another time I sat down with a man and bought the property he was selling for much less than the asking price—even though he had refused to sell it to me! Was it my own talents or was it Christ working through me?

These things have happened countless times. What do I need to do for God in return for the many blessings He pours into my life? Jesus answered that question when He said, "The work of God is this: to believe in the one he has sent" (John 6:29). Having faith in Jesus is all I need to do!

Then, as if that freedom weren't enough, the very faith that I have "is the gift of God" (Ephesians 2:8). In short, there is absolutely nothing that I can give to warrant Him, His kindness, or His love toward me. And even what I can give Him— my faith—is a gift from Him!

That's the grace of God! Every detour away from God's grace will end up where you don't want to be. *I'll take His grace any day!*

DETOUR #3—WANTING TO BE LIKE CHRIST

For years, my greatest desire as I journeyed with Christ was to be like Him. I wanted to love like He loved, give like He gave, and serve like He served. I desired to imitate Him in every area. And why not? After all, He is the perfect example.

Though this is a noble goal and sounds very "Christian," it is not biblical. God does not want me to be like Christ, and for several reasons:

1. It is impossible for me to be perfect like Christ.

2. To want to be like Christ excludes Him from working in my life.

3. It leads me toward good works as a means of salvation, which is unbiblical and religious.

4. It sets me up for a fall.

Not only is trying to imitate Christ an effort in futility, but it is also wrong. I knew salvation required that I accept Christ by faith, but trying to be like Christ seemed an appropriate goal as a Christian. What I didn't realize was that Christ placed His life *into me* so that He could live His life *through me*. My walk with Christ has nothing to do with me imitating Him and everything to do with me walking, living, and breathing *with* Him. Scripture says, "We have come to share in Christ" (Hebrews 3:14).

It doesn't even need to be my goal to do what He did. I can't do what He did! Nobody can. Where does that leave me? It leaves me in a better position than I could have ever imagined! The fact that God does not want me to be like Christ frees my heart, mind, and soul from the shackles of performance and religion.

On the detour of wanting to be like Christ, I thought trying to be Christlike was what I needed to do, *but because of God's grace I don't need to do anything!* It takes some getting used to, realizing that I am not under pressure to do anything to please God or to prove my Christianity, but that is the reality of grace.

The fact is, as I walk with Christ and allow Him to work in and through me, I end up acting like Him anyway! I don't need to *try* to be like Him—I *am* like Him because He is in me.

- - - - - - -

The longer I walk with Christ, the more I understand His grace, the more I change, and the more I see what He intends for me to be and to do. Have I arrived? *By no stretch of the imagination!*

Walking with Christ is a lifelong journey that never ends —and I don't want it to end!

FINDING GOD'S WILL FOR YOUR LIFE

I'll be honest—finding God's will for my life was not easy. It wasn't that God was keeping it a secret or that I wasn't willing to follow Him, but rather that *I just didn't know how to blend His will into my life and make it work.*

"Full speed ahead" has always been my approach. It is my temperament and training to jump in with everything I have to accomplish a goal. Add in my mother's Scottish determination and nothing could stand in my way! That may explain why I won every sales competition I ever entered.

But I found that with my inner drive and natural gifts, it was easy to leave God out of the picture. I can set any goal and achieve it, but that may or may not be God's will.

Before I could focus on accomplishing God's will, I needed to first learn how to handle myself.

HIS WILL, MY WILL, AND ME

The practicality of being goal oriented, doggedly determined, and highly motivated makes for an interesting combination. It has its benefits and its drawbacks, but so it is with
every person. Some have an intellectual conflict, a power conflict, an authority conflict, or an insecurity conflict. Add these
to the fact that all Christians have a conflict between their own
wants and the wants of the Holy Spirit that lives inside of them
and you have more than enough obstacles to try to prevent you
from accomplishing God's will.

It wasn't easy for me to turn my will over to God. Mentally
and emotionally I could do it, but reality was another matter.
About half the time I was seeking God's will; the other half I
was not.

When a great business idea of mine would go up in smoke,
I would at least accept responsibility for my actions (my parents had taught me that one very well), but I would kick myself
later for not asking God for His will first. It was a process of my
submitting my will to His.

A good friend once confided in me, "I have struggled with
finding God's will for my life because I wanted Him to help me
with my will rather than me helping Him with His will."

The more we see ourselves for who we are—*limited in every
respect*—and the more we see Him for who He is—*unlimited in
every respect*, the less we will demand our own way.

The answers began to fall into place when I started to daily
apply the Scriptures to my prayer life, my thought life, and
then to my physical life. The basis of everything is Matthew
6:33, which states, "Seek first his kingdom and his righteousness, and all these things will be given to you as well." I follow
that up with the first two commandments: having no other
gods before God and not making any idols (Exodus 20:3–4).

I would also pray at the beginning of every day for wisdom,
then proceed as if He answered my prayer, trusting that what

Proverbs 3:6 says is true: "in all your ways acknowledge him and he will make your paths straight."

Throughout the process of preparing myself to know and accomplish the will of God, I learned how to find His will.

GOD'S WILL FOR YOUR LIFE

How can you find the will of God for your life? There are more books, recordings, and seminars on the topic than ever in human history, yet the same question continues to surface.

Why is that? The reason, at least from my perspective, is that there are seven interrelated parts (like pieces in a puzzle) in our pursuit of God's will that must be assembled *and most people haven't put all seven pieces together.* It isn't any more complex than that!

If you leave one out, your puzzle is incomplete, so don't even think about leaving one out!

#1—BIG PLANS

You must *believe* that God does have a plan for your life because you are in His family. It's as simple as that. He created you, adopted you into His family, and made you a son or daughter (Ephesians 1:5). And as an heir, He has big plans for you!

#2—HIS WILL

To sincerely *desire* to do His will means that you need to set the goal to include God in every aspect of your goal-setting process. This requires a heart attitude that says, "Not my will but Yours be done."

Then listen, watch, wait patiently, and let Him show you His will *as you go about your daily routine.* A specific answer might come through advice from a respected friend or from a happenstance meeting on a street corner. It's happened to me!

What is interesting is that while I'm seeking His will, He is working on my character. Then when I'm walking in His will, He continues to work on my character. This leads me to believe that whether I'm seeking His will or "in" His will, I win.

#3—HIS WORD

You need to continuously search His Word (the Bible) for direction. As a result, you will continually be pointed in the

> IT'S ALL RIGHT TO BE STUBBORN AS A MULE, BUT ONLY WHEN GOD IS IN CONTROL.

right direction—toward Christ! As you do this, God will equip you to know and live His perfect plan for your life.

#4—ACCEPT RESPONSIBILITY

I've heard all types of prayers, from, "God, what color should I paint my bedroom?" to "Should I take my umbrella with me today?" Despite the earnestness of such prayers, I personally don't think God cares in the slightest about the color of our room or whether we carry an umbrella or not.

Practically speaking, if you don't like the color you painted your bedroom, then paint it another color, and if it rains and you don't have your umbrella, you will get wet. Asking God what to do in every little detail is not faith at all—it is immaturity, evidence that a person would rather be told what to do than to take responsibility for his or her own actions.

> ASKING GOD WHAT TO DO IN EVERY LITTLE DETAIL IS NOT FAITH AT ALL—IT IS IMMATURITY.

Real faith is when you don't know exactly what to do but you walk in the wisdom and knowledge you have, believing that God is directing your steps. That is what faith is all about.

By being overly concerned about being exactly "in the middle" of God's will, we can easily become extreme and destroy our relevancy to those around us. There is a commonsense balance here somewhere that comes with experience.

#5—GIVE UP CONTROL

To give up control does not mean that you submit to another person and do exactly what he or she says; nor does it mean you wait around for God to tell you what to do. Rather, it means that you are "leadable," which entails being:

A. in motion (moving toward your goals)

B. willing to do what He tells you to do (humble and teachable)

Trust that God will communicate through His Holy Spirit that dwells inside of you to lead you. (In essence, you have a "built-in guidance system" to get you where you need to go.)

> IF YOU MAKE A MISTAKE, LEARN FROM IT SO YOU DON'T HAVE TO DO IT AGAIN, THEN MOVE ON.

"What if I mess it up?" people often ask. God is big enough to lead you and He is big enough to fix anything you might break along the way. Don't put pressure on yourself to be perfect. If you make a mistake, learn from it so you don't have to do it again. Then move forward—toward Him.

You can always rest assured that "all things work together for good to those who love God, to those who are the called according to His purpose" (Romans 8:28 NKJV).

#6—EVEN IN HARD TIMES

Walking in the will of God is intended to be a lifelong journey, as is the fact that *God will continue to lead you.* He never takes vacations, siestas, or the weekend off. He is always watching over you and directing your steps—even during the hard times.

Sometimes God stops us from doing something that we want because He knows it would be wrong for us. Years ago I wanted to go into a certain business and did everything I could think of to make it a reality. I confess that I didn't ask what God's will was for me; I simply proceeded, but God kept slamming the door shut!

As I spent more time in the Scriptures and in prayer, God began to reveal to me what His perfect plans were. My big plans turned out to be miniscule in comparison to His, and the door He opened no one could close, just like His Word that says, "I have placed before you an open door that no one can shut" (Revelation 3:8).

I can honestly say that I could never in a million years have imagined what God had planned for me—and I have a pretty good imagination! He has directed me every step along the way, through thick and thin, through highs and lows, so much so that I've had to recognize: "a man's steps are directed by the LORD. *How then can anyone understand his own way?*" (Proverbs 20:24, emphasis mine).

#7—TRUST HIM

The last piece of the puzzle, though equally as important as all the others, is often the most difficult to apply. It is summed up in this: Do we really trust God?

I've been through things, both very good and very bad, that could have hurt me (my wife, family, business, etc.) had I not trusted and obeyed God.

> "IN HIS WILL IS OUR PEACE."
> —Dante

Other times He has told me to do things that didn't make sense when I put them up against conventional wisdom, but I have learned to trust Him despite what I or others might say or think. Through it all, He has shown Himself trustworthy— *every time!*

It is my strong belief that God has something special in store for you! I believe He will not only take care of you, but that His will for your life is far greater than you could ever ask or imagine.

Just you wait and see.

IS THERE A GUARANTEE?

How can you guarantee that you will walk in God's will? There is only one way: Make Him Lord of your life and place your will under His. From there, He can direct the desires He gives you or has already given you.

By giving each of us dreams and visions for our future, He is taking a chance that we won't run ahead and try to accomplish them ourselves. But if we truly want to do His will (and are smart enough to realize we can't do it on our own), then we need to do it His way.

I finally got it through my aggressive head that if I wanted to accomplish His will, I had to get in step with Him. For me, it meant I needed to slow down, be patient, and walk in His wisdom. As I did, I found myself right where I needed to be.

WHY ISN'T THE WILL OF GOD INSTANT, EASY, AND PAINLESS?

Finding the will of God is obviously important, but our tendency is to always think in terms of what we *do* for God. After all, it's His will we seek, which means accomplishing His will is our goal.

It would be a whole lot easier if God would simply give each of us an outline of our future with specific directions written out in numerical order. *But if He wanted robots, He would have created robots.*

Instead, He equips us with our own free will because He wants a relationship with every one of us. There can be no relationship when there is no free will. When we choose to submit our will to His, He loves it.

> **YOU HAVE A DESTINY. YOU DON'T HAVE TO BEG GOD TO BRING IT TO PASS. JUST RELAX! SEEK TO KNOW HIM BETTER AND OBEY HIS VOICE—*AND YOU WILL FIND YOURSELF SMACK DAB IN THE CENTER OF HIS WILL!***

When He blesses us with peace and fulfillment and more than we could imagine, we love it (and so does He).

The bottom line is that God is really more concerned with your heart than He is with what you might do for Him. That is why finding and accomplishing His will is a lifelong pursuit—because He is working on you (who you are) at the same time He is working through you (what you do for Him).

In *Experiencing God,* Henry T. Blackaby and Claude V. King wrote, "We need to first know Him before we know His will." That is because God is more interested in a relationship with us than in anything we could ever do for Him.

His will for your life is only part of the whole picture, so enjoy the journey and the means by which He speaks to you, because the end result will surpass your greatest expectations!

HOW I WANT TO BE REMEMBERED

—WHAT THE BOTTOM
LINE REALLY LOOKS
LIKE UP CLOSE

There is an old saying that if you want to know what people will say about you when you are gone, write your own epitaph now and then live that way! That isn't a bad idea.

What would your epitaph say? How do you want to be remembered?

Epitaphs are usually one-liners that capture the essence of a person's life. Since there is no rule that says you can't have more than one epitaph, here are thirteen (my favorite number) epitaphs about how I would like to be remembered:

1. HE LOVED GOD FIRST
   (Without God, I am nothing and have nothing of value to pass on through my legacy. I love Him because He loves me more than I can imagine and because of all He has done for me.)

2. HE LOVED HIS FAMILY AND EXTENDED FAMILY
(You can't ask for anything more precious than family. They are there with you when things are going well and when things are going bad. I love my family!)

> **WE WILL BE REMEMBERED FOR WHAT WE ACTUALLY DO, NOT WHAT WE WISH WE HAD DONE.**

3. HE LOVED HIS FRIENDS
(I still write to my grammar and high school principals who are in their eighties, many of my former school teachers, schoolmates, military friends, and other individuals who have shaped my life.)

4. HE WAS A GIVER
(My long-time friend and associate Gladys Hudson used to say I take it for granted that seeing a need defines my opportunity to help. Of course I do! Meeting needs is my opportunity to give back, to help, to serve, to bless—*and besides, it's a whole lot of fun!*)

5. HE WAS AN ENCOURAGER
(I want people to walk away feeling more encouraged and more excited about life than before they saw me.)

6. HE FORGAVE!
(There is nothing in the world so important that I can't forgive another person. The freedom and liberty that forgiveness brings is indescribable, and I do all I can to liberate others as well.)

7. HE KEPT HIS WORD
(I believe that keeping my word is of utmost importance. I have made promises many years ago that are written in my will—when I die, my promises will still be kept.)

8. HE HONORED GOD WITH HIS LIFE
(My hope is that everything I do in life will be a testament of God's goodness. Scripture says that He is worthy

"to receive glory and honor and power" (Revelation 4:11).
God deserves to be honored with everything I am and
ever will be.)

9. HE ALWAYS HAD A POSITIVE ATTITUDE
(My "attitude should be the same as that of Christ Jesus"
(Philippians 2:5), which I believe includes: never giving
up, serving, loving, giving, seeing the best in others, and
much, much more.)

10. HE WAS NOT ASHAMED OF THE GOSPEL OF JESUS CHRIST
(I recognize that everything is His and that everything I
am is a result of Him! I try to advance the gospel of Christ
through my words, actions, and financial support.)

11. HE WAS A ROLE MODEL
(My objective is to prepare my children and grandchildren for the best future imaginable—in every sense of
the word—and this means always pushing them closer
and closer to Jesus Christ!)

12. HE CONTRIBUTED TO HIS COMMUNITY
(I purposefully help my community and encourage others to catch the same vision—many more people are
helped that way. Our foundations help many local charities and people in need.)

13. HE CONSISTENTLY HELPED OTHERS
(A handout is one thing, but a hand up is so much better.
A gift or act of service once a year is nice, but change
usually comes through long-term help—I believe it is the
least I can do.)

WHAT OTHERS SAY ABOUT YOU

I recognize that the true test of an epitaph is what others
actually say about you. As much as we would like great things
said about us, it all comes down to the reality of our actions. What

we do has a longer lasting impact than anything we might say.

> "THE GOLDEN RULE IS OF NO USE TO YOU WHATSO-EVER UNLESS YOU REALIZE THAT IT IS YOUR MOVE."
> —Dr. Frank Crane

Over the years I have kept the thank-you notes, letters, and cards that people have sent me. Their comments encourage me more than words can say, and though many claim to have been blessed by something I did, *I can say with all honesty that I was more blessed in the giving than they were in the receiving.*

Here is a sampling of the kind notes I have received:

"You do not know me, and I have never met you, but you have given me the greatest opportunity to continue my education. I would not have been able to go to school without your help. I could never let you know by words or expression how much your help means to me."
　　　　—Wendy

"Thank you so very much for the $500 donation when our house burned. That was truly the nicest thing anybody ever did for us."
　　　　—Sandy

"Thank you for all the material on cancer. I've been trying to read as much as possible on diets as well as alternative treatments. Today I started the third chemo treatment in a series of six. One must try to keep a positive attitude. Sunday I started to read again the book you sent. Please keep us in your prayers."
　　　　—Millie

"Thanks so much for your help to go to camp. It was awesome."
　　　　—Kristin

"We received our prayer books and the kids their 'champion' program also last week. The kids were so excited I let them go to bed listening to the first tape. I'm trying to read through my prayer book every night and know it will become more and more a part of my life. Thank you so much."
　　　　—Bob

"Thank you for your generous support of our Development Department start-up. Our development director has had a tremendous effect already on our finances. Your 'seed money' is already producing much fruit for the Kingdom."

—Dean

"I want to begin by saying how much I appreciate your generous donation to my recent mission trip to Algiers, Spain. It enabled me to have a life-changing experience that I will not forget."

—Jared

"In 1988 you generously paid an attorney to save some property for me, and to keep my youngest daughter out of jail, for which I am forever grateful. Thanks to you, she turned her life around, and is a much changed person."

—Sarah

"I want you to know that I read and review every article, book, and tape you send my way for personal and spiritual development. I am deeply moved that you care enough to send such materials to your employees."

—Amy

> "ONE OF THE MOST AMAZING THINGS EVER SAID ON THIS EARTH IS JESUS' STATEMENT: 'HE THAT IS GREATEST AMONG YOU SHALL BE YOUR SERVANT.' NOBODY HAS ONE CHANCE IN A BILLION OF BEING THOUGHT REALLY GREAT AFTER A CENTURY HAS PASSED EXCEPT THOSE WHO HAVE BEEN THE SERVANTS OF ALL. THAT STRANGE REALIST FROM BETHLEHEM KNEW THAT."
>
> —Harry Emerson Fosdick, D.D.

"I don't know how to thank you for what you have done [paying for her son to attend Bible college]. I don't know how to thank God either, but I know you are working together on this. How can I thank you for doing something so huge. I will be grateful always. Every time I think about it I cry… Thank you from the bottom of my heart."

—Inez

In all of these letters, I can't help but stop and think about the future that these individuals have. I am honored to play just a little part in helping make their lives a little better.

They may be thankful, but I am more thankful. They may cry, but I've cried more. They may laugh, but I've laughed more. They may be excited, but I'm even more excited. Helping always does me more good than it does them—always!

In fact, I should be the one writing letters to them!

HOW WILL WE BE REMEMBERED IN 100 YEARS?

Not one of us will be here in 100 years. Few will argue with that, but the question for me is, "What will people be saying about me 100 years from now?"

A long-time friend of mine, Harold Keown Sr. is perhaps one of the most thoughtful and encouraging people I have ever met. One hundred years from now, he will probably not be remembered for having the world's largest collection of personal-development books, though that is true, but for his kind treatment of other people.

I know Harold and could talk for hours about him, but I will never know my great-grandparents who lived 100 years ago. What were their hopes and dreams? What did they believe in? What did they want to accomplish? What motivated them?

I was told quite a bit about my mother's family, but unfortunately for me, my father tried to purposefully erase his past. There are entire portions of his life that he never told us about! I have since spent a lot of time and money trying to track down my father's side of the family. Though I learned a little, including

> THE SEEDS THAT WE SOW WILL CONTINUE TO TOUCH LIVES BECAUSE THE RIPPLE EFFECT OF GOODNESS IS MULTIPLIED MANY TIMES AS THE YEARS GO BY.
> —Wanda Henderson

the fact that the past ten generations on both sides of my family were Christians (now *that* is a legacy!), I recognize that much more was lost than I will ever know.

My hope is that my great-grandchildren will have the answers I never did. We owe it to those who come after us to answer the questions we wish we could have asked our ancestors *and* to put those answers in book, video, or some other format that they will be able to use. The place to start is deciding how we want to be remembered.

ONE MORE CHANCE

When I was twelve years old and in the Boy Scouts, my best friend, Billy Farnham, and I went camping with 3000 other Scouts in the mountains of California. During the night Billy lit a candle inside our tent (perhaps because he was scared) and then fell back asleep. The candle ignited his sleeping bag and he burned to death—but I escaped without a scratch. I promised Billy's father, who was also the scoutmaster, that I would grow up to be a Scout for both of us, but that did not stop me from wondering, "Why him and not me?"

We don't always get a second chance. As adults, we often miss what is most important in life until it is too late. I know many people who could easily interchange their name for Joe's in the following story:

> **"REASON, TOO LATE PERHAPS, MAY CONVINCE YOU OF THE FOLLY OF MISSPENDING TIME."**
>
> —George Washington

On his deathbed, Joe's family asked him what he wished he had done while he still could. Instead of listing all the things he had spent years pursuing and dreaming about, such as the bigger house, the ultimate job, more investments, better vacations, etc., Joe's wish list was short and simple.

He wished he had spent more time together as a family, gone to Europe with Marge, his wife, gone to his kids' ballgames, taken his grandkids out of school for lunch more often, and not worked as much. In everything he said, the only reference to work was wishing he had done less of it.

Isn't it interesting that in life's most trying times, what is most important instantly comes to the surface and what is not as important is suddenly inconsequential? Sadly, most people do not get another chance because they come to the revelation when it is too late.

A long time ago *I purposed that I would do today what I would wish I had done tomorrow.* This perspective has allowed me to enjoy many special times with other people. Not long ago I took the day off from work to spend time with three of my granddaughters, four-wheeling on my ranch and skipping stones in a creek. They said we had a "blast," but I don't know who had more fun, them or me.

> "SIMPLE WALKS WITH MY FATHER AROUND THE BLOCK ON SUMMER NIGHTS WHEN I WAS A CHILD DID WONDERS FOR ME AS AN ADULT."
>
> —Andy Rooney

I know a father of two young children who recently went through his parent's 8-mm film collection, having it converted into VHS format. He told me, "The entire collection of film was a mere twenty minutes long, and even more disappointing was the fact that I found a *blank* roll of 8-mm film!" The potential was there many years earlier to capture more of his life history, but the opportunity was gone. It would never be.

I don't think we can afford to lose a single moment—life is just too short! I've walked away from plane crashes and other near misses too many times to ever take a new day for granted. I want to make the most of every day because tomorrow is not guaranteed. That is why one of my favorite sayings is "carpe diem," which means "seize the day."

HABITS THAT HELP YOU "SEIZE THE DAY"

I believe there are certain habits that when fostered will enable us to live life to its fullest, making the most of every opportunity. These habits are not personality traits! Rather, they are little choices that we internalize into habits.

Here are thirteen of my favorite habits that help me seize each day:

1. BE AN INVERTED PARANOID—Believe that the whole world is conspiring to do only good things to me.

2. BE A QUICK FORGIVER—I know I have been forgiven for much, therefore I want to forgive much. Besides, I don't have time to waste in unforgiveness.

3. BE OPTIMISTIC—Believing the best in people and circumstances is a sure way to find the best. Pessimists usually find what they are looking for!

4. BE THANKFUL—Always giving thanks keeps my eyes on God as my provider and a smile on my face. Thankful people are also much more fun to be around.

5. BE AN ENCOURAGER—Encouragers make me feel better, stronger, and more capable of accomplishing my dreams. I want to do the same with every person I meet.

> DO TODAY WHAT YOU WILL WISH YOU HAD DONE TOMORROW.

6. BE SPONTANEOUS—Take advantage of situations and circumstances. I've met people in every conceivable place who ended up dramatically impacting my life, or vice versa. I have a sense of urgency and a do-it-now attitude.

7. BE A GIVER—I tell people, "If I can be of any service to you or your children, anytime, anywhere, anyplace, just

call." It gives me a chance to be a giver, and that's my greatest joy! The only problem is that they don't call often enough.

8. BE POSITIVE—Not enough can ever be said about the benefits of having a positive attitude. Being positive has the potential of turning the worst situations into victories.

9. SMILE A LOT AND LAUGH AT LIFE—Adversity is a stepping stone, not a roadblock at the end of the road, and mistakes are opportunities to learn, not signs of failure. Why not laugh in the midst of challenges that are good for you?

10. LIVE LIFE WITH ENTHUSIASM—I live only once, so why not give it my all? I believe I can do far more than I think I can, and enthusiasm helps me try harder.

11. ENJOY LIFE—I enjoy life. For many years I have collected 1936 Fords, chased down our family genealogy, and worked to establish our company library of personal development books. It has brought enjoyment to me and to many other people as well.

12. FIND A HOBBY YOU ENJOY—Hiking, scuba diving, tennis, golf, swimming, biking, and fishing are a few of my hobbies. Then no matter where I am, I have something I enjoy doing.

> "IF YOU ARE FORTUNATE, SOMEONE WITH MORAL AUTHORITY WILL ASK YOU THAT QUESTION [HOW DO YOU WANT TO BE REMEMBERED] EARLY ENOUGH IN YOUR LIFE SO THAT YOU WILL CONTINUE TO ASK IT AS LONG AS YOU LIVE."
>
> —Peter F. Drucker

13. LOOK FOR PEOPLE TO HELP—I get up every morning excited about the person I might help that day. The actual help will take many different forms, but when I'm actively looking for someone, I seldom miss.

ANSWERING LIFE'S FINAL QUESTIONS

Nate Meleen, a long-time friend who was also a neighbor when I was a boy, once told me, "My life's goal is that when I die, not one thing God has planned for me will be left unfinished." Now *that* is a great perspective!

When accomplishing God's will and hearing "Well done, good and faithful servant!" (Matthew 25:21) is our goal, questions like "What do you wish you had done while you still could?" and "What do you want your epitaph to say?" will answer themselves.

When all is said and done, one final question remains: "How do I want to be remembered?" The answer you give will be your legacy.

EPILOGUE

When all is said and done, each of us will leave only four things behind:

1. MEMORIES—thoughts that others have of us

2. SOUVENIRS—proof of our existence

3. TROPHIES—records of our achievements

4. LEGACIES—everything you are and possess today

Eventually, memories will fade and souvenirs and trophies will disappear (be lost, stolen, or sold at garage sales). I still have my father's carpentry tools, my mother's diplomas, and countless black and white photos, but sentimental value can only go so far. What has impacted me the most has been what my parents left me through their legacy, be it social, physical, mental, spiritual, financial, or emotional.

I too want to leave a lasting legacy through what I leave

behind, but I have learned from firsthand experience that a legacy may take years to prepare and years to receive. It is not an instant process. This makes passing on a legacy of vital importance.

THE PROCESS OF PASSING ON YOUR LEGACY

Enjoying the memories, souvenirs, and trophies is of course not wrong, but our focus should always be on leaving a legacy that will continue for generations. Dennis Peacocke, president and founder of Strategic Christian Services,[12] points out that "lasting wealth is multigenerational and is oriented toward the long-run, not the short-run." That is why generational wealth often disappears in two or three generations. It isn't stolen; it's mismanaged . . . and so it is with a legacy.

When King Solomon, the world's wisest and possibly richest man in all of history, died, his throne passed down to his son Rehoboam. Despite the wisdom, riches, and fame of his father and grandfather (King David, "a man after his [God's] own heart," –1 Samuel 13:14), King Rehoboam made a series of decisions that sent his kingdom into revolt.

> "A LEGACY WILL TRANSCEND TO THOSE WE WILL NEVER SEE. THAT CAUSES ME TO HAVE A MIND-SET THAT IS BEYOND DEATH. MOST PEOPLE ARE ATTEMPTING TO SURVIVE DEATH; IF THAT IS ALL, DEATH HAS ALREADY WON!"
>
> —Ron Hyatt, pastor

The overworked people of Israel gathered together soon after he became king and begged for mercy, but Rehoboam rejected the advice of the elders and listened to his friends. "My father laid on you a heavy yoke," he told them. "I will make it even heavier" (1 Kings 12:10–11).

From that day forward, Rehoboam was at war with his own people—and war continued throughout the entire reign of his son as well! The vast majority of the prosperity, blessing, wisdom, and peace that had been part of the family legacy was gone.

We, of course, claim that we would not make the same mistakes that Rehoboam made, but his actions that merely reflected what was in his heart are commonplace today. In his heart, he:

> **EVERYONE LEAVES A LEGACY—*WHETHER YOU HAVE CHILDREN OR NOT.***

- believed that character and integrity were not important

- was proud, selfish, demanding, and unkind

- was not humble, teachable, or accountable

- craved wealth, fame, and power

Had King Solomon better prepared his son for his role as king, I believe history would be different. Or perhaps it was King David who failed to train Solomon for the throne? Regardless of who was at fault, the fact remains that the potential for passing on a good legacy was lost.

Throughout history, many great kingdoms and empires have been lost in the generations that followed, but this does not have to be. We have the opportunity to change the future by the legacy we leave behind.

THE "HOW TO" OF PASSING IT ON

As you know, there are no guarantees or "ten easy steps" to ensuring that your legacy will pass successfully to the next generation. Granted, there are numerous things you should and should not do, such as:

SHOULD DO	SHOULD NOT DO
• leave room for mistakes	• compare what you did to what they do
• encourage them in every area	• expect perfection
• teach them to think long-term	• pressure them to succeed
• train them to trust God	• expect them to be just like you

Despite such commonsense wisdom, the absolute best "how to" is still active participation. This involves a combination of equipping, training, preparing, and living by example.

I believe we all equally possess the ability to leave a life-changing legacy with those who come after us. It is my sincere hope that the previous Legacy Keys have helped you in the establishing of your legacy, because no matter what you do, the day will inevitably come when your legacy becomes someone else's legacy.

NOBODY SAID IT WOULD BE EASY

Though anything is possible, nobody said it would be easy to prepare and train those who come after you to receive and live out their legacy. Scripture says that "a good man leaves an inheritance for his children's children" (Proverbs 13:22). Besides being something we wish our grandparents had done for us, it also makes common sense. However, to do so will cost you and me something right now.

Admittedly, an inheritance for our children's children covers much more than money, but *the principle is that we will pay a price today for something that our children and their children will enjoy in the future.* When you live like this with the future in mind, you almost feel like you are living for someone else. In essence, *you are!*

The price we pay is a natural part of leaving a legacy. In *The Road Less Traveled,* author Scott Peck wisely stated, "Life is difficult. This is a great truth, one of the greatest truths. It is a great truth because once we truly see this truth, we transcend it. Once we truly understand and accept it—then life is no longer difficult. Because once it is accepted, the fact that life is difficult no longer matters."

> "WHEN WE BUILD, LET US THINK THAT WE BUILD FOREVER. LET IT NOT BE FOR PRESENT DELIGHT, NOT FOR PRESENT USE ONLY; LET IT BE SUCH WORK AS OUR DESCENDANTS WILL THANK US FOR."
>
> —John Ruskin (1819–1900)

Similarly, when we understand and accept the fact that leaving a legacy is not easy and that it will cost us, then, as Peck says, "it no longer matters." It all becomes worth it!

Imagine if those who came before us had taken seriously the potential of a legacy! Life would most likely be very different. But whether you received such a legacy or not, it does not matter.

How much or how little we were given, whether mental, physical, financial, emotional, social, or spiritual, does not matter. Scripture says, "Better a little with the fear of the LORD than great wealth with turmoil" and "Better a meal of vegetables where there is love than a fattened calf with hatred" (Proverbs 15:16–17).

Leaving a good legacy is limited only by the limitations we place on ourselves. The legacy you leave behind could someday change the world!

WHEN IT COMES RIGHT DOWN TO IT

How much we have, whom we know, what our profession is, or how many foundations we have started for the sake of charity will have absolutely no value when our life is over. The only thing that will matter is whether or not we have a personal relationship with Jesus Christ. I believe that everyone, Christian and non-Christian alike, will make a temporary stop at the same place: the feet of God.

> **"NOTHING WORTH DOING IS COMPLETED IN OUR LIFETIME."**
> —Reinhold Niebuhr

There, Scripture says, "every tongue [will] confess that Jesus Christ is Lord, to the glory of God the Father" (Philippians 2:11).

From there, our paths will separate.

While we still have breath, let us prepare for our eternity—and the eternity of those who come after us—by coming to the saving knowledge of Jesus Christ.

That is the ultimate legacy.

REVIEW
QUESTIONS

PART I—WHERE EVERY GOOD LEGACY BEGINS

LEGACY KEY #1—LOVE—WHERE EVERY GOOD LEGACY BEGINS

- ◆ Which of the three—love of self, love of others, or love of God—is most difficult for you? Why is that the case?

- ◆ What are several practical ways in which you can demonstrate the love that you find most difficult to give?

- ◆ Have you ever experienced the magnitude of God's love for you? How did that impact your life?

- ◆ What steps are you taking to ensure that love will be a part of your legacy?

LEGACY KEY #2—WE ALL STAND ON LEVEL GROUND

- ◆ Do you really believe that everyone stands on level ground?

- ◆ Have you ever traveled to a country where your language, culture, and color are not dominant? (I recommend it!)

- ◆ Did your parents, teachers, etc., teach you that we all stand on level ground? How did that affect you?

- ◆ What will you do to ensure that your legacy includes this important truth?

LEGACY KEY #3—TELLING OTHERS ABOUT YOUR FAITH

- Have you been pressured to become a Christian or to tell others about Christ? How did that affect you?

- What is it about a personal relationship with Jesus Christ that makes it the ultimate legacy to leave behind?

- Which of your talents and interests might be the perfect way to tell others about Christ?

- How can telling others about your faith become a practical part of the legacy you leave?

LEGACY KEY #4—THE JOURNEY OF PRAYER

- What is prayer and why do you pray?

- Do you honestly believe that God hears your prayers and will answer them? Why?

- When did prayer gain more meaning in your life?

- How will you practically mix prayer with your legacy?

PART II—ATTITUDES FOR LIVING THE CHRISTIAN LIFE

LEGACY KEY #5—ATTITUDE IS EVERYTHING

- How do you see yourself: negatively or positively? Why?

- What did you do to see yourself and the world around you in the way that you do?

- If there is an attitude in any area of your life that you are not pleased with, what are you doing to change it?

- What is the best way to pass your positive attitude on to those who come after you?

LEGACY KEY #6—LIVING LIFE WITH AN ATTITUDE OF GRATITUDE

- How do you foster an attitude of gratitude?

- What is it that you are most grateful/thankful for?

- What benefits do you believe are associated with an attitude of gratitude? Are you a beneficiary?

- What are you doing to instill gratitude into your life and into your legacy?

LEGACY KEY #7—MIRRORING YOUR POSITIVE SELF-IMAGE

- How would you describe your self-image?

- How did you gain the self-image you currently have?

- If your self-image is not as positive as you would like it to be, what steps are you taking to increase your self-image?

- What steps are you taking to bolster the positive self-image of those who will receive your legacy?

PART III—BEING TRUE TO YOURSELF
LEGACY KEY #8—CHOICES AND CONSEQUENCES

- If you were the brunt of someone's bad choice, what have you done differently so that you won't make the same mistake they did?

- Does the word *consequences* have a positive or negative ring to you? How does this perception affect you?

- How do you use the principle of "by saying 'yes' to one thing, you are automatically saying 'no' to another" to your advantage?

- What will you include in your legacy concerning choices and consequences that you wish you had been given when you were young?

LEGACY KEY #9—THE RISE AND FALL OF DISCIPLINE

- ◆ Do you agree that discipline is as important as food, air, and water for success? Why?

- ◆ Is there room in your life for a little more discipline? If so, what are you doing to implement it?

- ◆ Where did you learn the discipline that you now utilize on a daily basis?

- ◆ What plans are you making to pass on this discipline you now enjoy?

LEGACY KEY #10—MY WORD IS MY BOND

- ◆ What is the difference between a promise you make verbally and a promise you make in writing?

- ◆ Is there anyone you know who keeps *every* promise he or she makes, regardless of how small or large it is?

- ◆ What practical steps do you take to ensure that the promises you make will be kept?

- ◆ Is your word as good as gold?

LEGACY KEY #11—INTEGRITY—IT'S ALL YOU ARE

- ◆ How would you describe a foundation of integrity?

- ◆ What are your top five favorite benefits of integrity?

- ◆ Is the person you admire most also a person of integrity? How are you positively impacted?

- ◆ What can you do to strengthen your legacy's foundation of integrity?

PART IV—MY WORK IS MY MINISTRY

LEGACY KEY #12—MY WORK IS MY MINISTRY

+ Do you see your work as your ministry? Why or why not?

+ How do you combine faith with works?

+ Have you found peace with doing what God has equipped you to do?

+ If you could do anything in life, what would it be? Why aren't you doing it now?

LEGACY KEY #13—IT'S ALL HIS BY RIGHT OF CREATION

+ What does it mean that we are stewards and never owners?

+ Why does the only challenge from God to "test me in this" (Malachi 3:10) pertain to the tithe?

+ Which area of stewardship is most difficult for you? What are you doing to remedy this?

+ How will your legacy practically include the principles of stewardship?

LEGACY KEY #14—THE ART OF MULTIPLYING YOUR GIFTS AND TALENTS

+ Which of your gifts and talents has multiplied the most?

+ Is there one aspect of multiplication that you find most difficult? If so, why?

+ What role do others play in your multiplication process?

+ Which of your multiplied gifts or talents has moved into a perpetual or permanent condition? Is this your goal?

LEGACY KEY #15—THE TRUE ROLE OF AN EMPLOYER

- What does it mean that the role of an employer is actually that of a servant?

- Have you ever had a servant-hearted employer? How did that affect your overall performance and job satisfaction?

- If you are currently an employer, what is it about being a servant that you find most difficult?

- How can you incorporate these principles of leading through service into your legacy?

PART V—SETTING LIFE IN ORDER

LEGACY KEY #16—PHILOSOPHY FOR LIVING

- How can a philosophy for living positively impact your life?

- What can you do to maximize this impact?

- What are the individual pieces that make up your personal philosophy for living?

- Which part of your philosophy for living is most important to you? How will this transfer through your legacy?

LEGACY KEY #17—THE IMPORTANCE OF PRIORITIES

- What are your priorities in descending order?

- Would you honestly say that you keep your priorities? Why or why not?

- Is there a certain priority that is difficult for you to keep as a priority? What steps are you taking to remedy this?

- How are you instilling the importance of priorities into those who will receive your legacy?

LEGACY KEY #18—TURNING YOUR DREAMS INTO REALITY

- What is goal setting?

- Why is goal setting so uncommon?

- How do you plan to incorporate the power of goal setting into your legacy?

- If you were able to reach every goal you set, where would you end up? So, what's stopping you?

PART VI—LIVING LIFE TO ITS FULLEST!

LEGACY KEY #19—FORGIVENESS! FORGIVENESS!

- Who was your model of forgiveness or unforgiveness? Did you follow his or her example?

- Is it more difficult to forgive others, yourself, or God? Why?

- Does your legacy include forgiveness that is grudgingly given or freely given?

- Have you accepted God's forgiveness for your sins? How does that affect your life?

LEGACY KEY #20—WAIT TO WORRY

- Do you worry? Why?

- What could be the most compelling reason(s) for you not to worry? Can you incorporate that into your life?

- How do you differentiate between a concern and a worry?

- What practical steps can you take to make your life worry-free?

LEGACY KEY #21—LAUGHING AT LIFE

- ◆ What do you most admire about people who don't take life too seriously? Why can't you do and be the same?

- ◆ Why do you believe laughter is such good medicine?

- ◆ What is the secret to being in touch with your emotions while maintaining the strong desire to look for humor in everything around you?

- ◆ How important is it to you to include laughter in your legacy?

PART VII—THE GREATEST LEGACY OF ALL

LEGACY KEY #22—THE GREATEST LEGACY OF ALL—KNOWING GOD

- ◆ Who took the time to teach you how to know God?

- ◆ Do you really know God (His heart and character) or do you mostly know about God?

- ◆ What is it about knowing God that makes it the greatest legacy of all?

- ◆ How will you enable those who receive your legacy to know God in a greater way than you do?

LEGACY KEY #23—WALKING WITH CHRIST

- ◆ What does it mean to "die to self"? How does this apply to walking with Christ?

- ◆ Why would God want to have a deeper relationship with us than a shepherd/sheep or king/servant relationship?

- ◆ What does it mean to be "saved by grace but live by works"? Does this apply to you?

- ◆ How does your legacy include the freeing truths of God's grace?

LEGACY KEY #24—FINDING GOD'S WILL FOR YOUR LIFE

* What is it about finding God's will that is difficult for most people?

* How do you find God's will for your life?

* What is the difference to you between Jesus as *Savior* and Jesus as *Lord*? Is He one, none, or both for you?

* How will you practically make knowing God's will part of your legacy?

LEGACY KEY #25—HOW I WANT TO BE REMEMBERED

* What would you like your epitaph to say?

* Are there things in your history that you would like to change? If so, why can't you start today?

* What is your secret to making "seize the day" a habit in your life?

* How do you want to be remembered?

ABOUT THE
AUTHOR

Paul J. Meyer began his insurance career (1948–57) immediately after military service and quickly became a top producer, leading two of the nation's largest life insurance companies. By age twenty-seven he had acquired a personal net worth of $1,000,000 from personal production and agency development.

He then spent two years (1958–59) as a sales executive with Word, Inc., of Waco, Texas, building a national sales organization and increasing its business by 1500 percent!

In 1960, Paul J. Meyer finally launched his dream business: Success Motivation Institute (SMI). Success Motivation International, Inc., Leadership Management (LMI) and Family Motivation International (FMI) followed soon after. All four firms were established for the purpose of helping people develop their full potential.

For these companies, the product line over the years has expanded to include twenty-four full-length courses and programs in leadership development and management training. All of these programs contain printed and recorded materials and have combined sales of more than two billion dollars worldwide, more than any other author in this field, dead or alive. He is considered by many to be the founder of the personal development industry.

The Meyer family also owns and operates thirty plus companies around the world, which include commercial construction, auto racing, farming, computer software, printing, and more.

Paul J. Meyer has been instrumental in founding five charitable foundations to promote education and serve youth, including Passport to Success, which has helped provide post-secondary education to more than 1000 economically disadvantaged youth. Many of the other twenty plus organizations and ministries across the nation and around the world that are supported by the Paul J. Meyer foundations are mentioned in this book.

Although Paul J. Meyer claims he officially retired at age seventy, he maintains his lifetime goal of doing all the good he can, for as many as he can, for as long as he can. As a result, his vision for the future has only increased.

"I have a legacy that I will someday leave behind," he says with passion, "and so do you!"

TRIBUTES TO
PAUL J. MEYER

"One of the greatest blessings in my fifty-one years in Christ has been witnessing God's power, love, and wisdom manifested through His servant Paul J. Meyer. God even worked through his parents to have them name him Paul. His stewardship and achievements are an inspiration to millions, and especially me."

CHARLIE T. JONES
AUTHOR OF *LIFE IS TREMENDOUS*

"I believe with all of my heart that God wants me to stay at home with my son . . . and your giving heart has made that possible. Someday, when my son is older, I will tell him about the man who taught me what the word *thankfulness* truly means. God has used you in my life—thank you for letting Him work through you."

MIKA, LEVI, AND JOSHUA HINSON

"As a business associate and personal friend, I have known Paul for more than thirty years. He is a man of influence and inspiration. His programs have not only helped me but also thousands of others in Japan to develop personally in every area of their lives. I personally appreciate his influence on my decision to become a Christian in 1987 and since then the rest of my family: my wife, my children, and my grandchildren. *Unlocking Your*

Legacy has positively influenced and challenged me with some fundamental questions on my personal walk with Christ. These treasures, ideas, and insights are more valuable to me than gold or silver."

HEI ARITA
PRESIDENT, PJM JAPAN CO., LTD.

"You have enabled Medical Exchange Programs to make a positive impact on the delivery of health care in Russia, Ukraine, and Romania. Your contributions have brought leading foreign physicians to Waco to learn the latest surgical techniques, medication, treatment regimens, and equipment in their specialty. Also, your financial support has enabled us to procure and to ship tons of valuable medical equipment and supplies to hospitals and clinics overseas. Your personal example of Christian stewardship and sacrificial giving has challenged and inspired countless thousands to increase their investment in kingdom work around the world."

DR. JOHN A. WOOD
PRESIDENT, MEDICAL EDUCATION FOUNDATION, INC.

"It was a great blessing when we met you and you were so gracious to provide us a scholarship to further our education. We are still amazed at how willing you were to help us when we were just strangers from another country. You loaned us a car and paid for our tuition and books when you hardly knew us. Your wise counsel and your personal encouragement have meant so much to us as we entered a new country and a new culture. You have given us hope which we haven't had for many years in our native Ukraine."

EUGENE AND INNA KLYMOVA

"Paul and Jane Meyer are outstanding examples of Christian stewards, and they are doing a wonderful job of passing their philosophy of giving on to future generations in their family."

PAUL PIPER SR.
FOUNDER, CHRIST IS OUR SALVATION FOUNDATION

"By any standard of measurement, Paul was a success when I first met him in 1974. During the years since that time, I have had opportunity to observe his amazing personal growth in every area of life. Spiritually, mentally, philosophically, and philanthropically, he continues to grow toward achieving his dreams to serve his Creator and his fellowman. The keys in *Unlocking Your Legacy* belong to all who will use them."

GLADYS HUDSON

"*Unlocking Your Legacy* reveals Paul's belief that the key to success is not self-improvement as much as selfless improvement."

CHARLES AND CORRIE DIXON, PASTOR
HARLINGEN, TEXAS

"Paul Meyer has lived his life by the instructions given in Matthew 25:34–45 and has used his worldly gifts to help "the least of these"—and inspired us all to do the same. I have been blessed to know this truly remarkable man."

JILL MCCALL

"Since we came to work for Paul J. Meyer, we have learned and experienced that the same statement the apostle Paul said to Timothy in Philippians 2:20, 'I have no one else like him, who takes genuine interest in your welfare,' applies to Paul J. Meyer. No matter what your status in life, he truly is a man who reaches out to you with genuine concern for your best interest."

BILL AND ALMA BUNTING
EXECUTIVE DIRECTORS OF SUMMERS MILL RETREAT &
CONFERENCE CENTER

"For many years, Paul Meyer has motivated people to succeed. Now he also motivates people to give—of themselves and their resources. He is leading people to leave the most amazing legacy of all, one that says, 'Because I lived, lives were changed for the better.' He has made a difference in the lives of thousands of people through our work at Friends for Life, and we are only one of the charities he supports. We all hope that one day we will look into the face of God and hear Him say, 'Well done.' I'm sure He will say that to Paul J. Meyer."

INEZ RUSSELL
FOUNDER, FRIENDS FOR LIFE

"Many Christians have boasted of what they would do for others if they had financial gain, only to see those promises vanish into mere tokenism when prosperity came. Paul Meyer is an exception. His compassion for the poor, unreached, and marginalized has driven his philanthropy far beyond 'safe' charity, personal attention, and public recognition. Paul has generously, humbly, and aggressively sought to make a difference in his own community for those who few even notice. On behalf of the voiceless to whom God has called us, Paul Meyer is not a rich man, but a fellow struggler seeking to be obedient to the Father who gifted him."

DR. JIMMY M. DORRELL

"Paul J. Meyer is a unique individual. He has not only discovered some important principles for life, but also lives them. He has touched thousands, no, probably millions of lives, including mine. The wisdom he shares and the Christian commitment he models may touch yours too."

LOUIS MCBURNEY, M.D.
FOUNDER, MARBLE RETREAT

"Paul J. Meyer practices what he preaches. His life has influenced and touched my life for more than two decades."

MICHAEL YOUSSEF, Ph.D.
HOST OF THE RADIO AND TV PROGRAM *LEADING THE WAY WITH DR. MICHAEL YOUSSEF*

"For thirty-two years, I have had the honor and privilege of knowing and working for Paul J. Meyer. I attribute my growth as a person and a Christian to him more than anyone else in my life. His positive attitude and hard work ethic have been contagious. His example has taught me to respect all people, regardless of race, creed, or religion. He has shown me that rewards are great for those who know and serve our Lord Jesus Christ."

LINDA PETERSON
EXECUTIVE ASSISTANT TO PAUL J. MEYER

"When I was seven years old, my father died. Although I was richly blessed with a wonderful mother and four sisters, there was a big void in my life. Having an intense imagination, I always believed I would meet someone like my father who truly cared about people, who wanted to help them develop their God-given potential, and who thought more highly of others than himself. It is amazing to me that not only have I met such a person, I am privileged to work for him and see firsthand this generous and kindhearted man in action. Paul J. Meyer is more than a boss to me. He is my friend, and the lessons on giving and helping others he has taught by example have left a major impression on my life and on the lives of my family as well. Thank you, Paul, for writing this book. May it serve to help others in their understanding of what is truly important in their lives."

KARON FREEMAN
EXECUTIVE ASSISTANT TO PAUL J. MEYER

"What Paul has written in this book is a wonderful example of the life he lives and the positive influence he has on the lives of others. No one has ever used their unique God-given talents for the good of the world more than Paul. These pages confirm that everything he has belongs to God and that he is a servant of Jesus Christ and a witness to His Word."

JOE E. BAXTER SR.

"Paul's rock-steady convictions come through *loud* and *clear* in this Christianity-for-everyday living tour de force. I am grateful to God for Paul's ability to not only write about his faith, but to teach by living it. He talks the talk *and* walks the walk."

TERRY WATLING

"Paul Meyer figured out how to be successful and never quit trusting God, even in the hard times. He knows how to use his genius to help others throughout the world and he wants his love of Jesus Christ to be reflected in his giving. We as readers have a rare chance to look inside the heart and mind of such a highly successful individual."

NELWYN REAGAN
CIVIC VOLUNTEER AND CONSULTANT

"Paul J. Meyer and I have been close friends for fifty years. There is no person I respect more. Paul's pattern of excellent values and giving is truly remarkable and is underlined by his dedicated Christian commitments. *Unlocking Your Legacy* will be an inspiration to those fortunate enough to learn its truths and values, written by a man of great faith, wisdom, and character."

WILLIAM C. ARMOR JR.

NOTES

1. Bill Nix's business and ministry at www.productability.com.

2. Man in the Mirror's website at www.maninthemirror.org.

3. the ongoing work of Project Hope at www.projecthope.org.

4. Crown Financial Ministries at www.crown.org.

5. Heifer Project International at www.heifer.org.

6. Christian Stewardship Association at www.stewardship.org.

7. Haggai Institute at www.haggai-institute.com.

8. Friends for Life at www.friendsforlifeonline.org.

9. MarketPlace Ministries at www.marketplaceministries.com.

10. FCCI at www.fcci.org.

11. Legacy Family Ministries at www.legacyfamily.org.

12. Strategic Christian Services at www.gostrategic.org.

ACKNOWLEDGMENTS

This book has been a long time in coming. To see it finally in print does wonders to my soul. It excites me to know the potential hidden within these pages. My hope and prayer is that it accomplishes more than I ever dreamed—*and I dream big!*

A lot of people helped to make this book a reality, and though I thank them here, the full impact of their assistance may not be seen for one hundred years! After all, this is a legacy we are talking about. They are:

Jane, my wife—your love and patience with me writing this, and every other goal and dream I've had amazes me.

Karon Freeman and Linda Peterson, the best executive assistants in the world—your attention to detail, long hours, and constant encouragement are appreciated every day!

Linda Wittig, the most serious teacher of children I know—thanks to your extensive research, many deletions and additions were made that helped this book in many ways.

Hei Arita, business associate from Japan and long-time friend—your views from another culture added another dimension and perspective to this book.

Dr. J. Clifton Williams—your forty-plus years of friendship, counsel, coaching and input have helped me in every area of life, this book included. Thank you!

Nate Meleen, long-time friend and professor at Oral Roberts University—your comments, incredibly insightful and on target, match your ability.

Brian Mast—your insights, ideas, suggestions, and edits have been invaluable in helping make this whole process a joy.

Dr. Winn Henderson, author and radio host—your eye for detail was of great benefit. Thank you.

Harold and Grace Keown, gifts to me and my family for many, many years—your knowledge and experience were an added blessing.

Byron Weathersbee, the most relevant minister to couples I have ever witnessed—thank you for helping carry on the legacy.

Jim Cole, my son's father-in-law and former pastor—your insights and wisdom were always helpful and warmly received.

You, the reader—it is an honor for me within these pages to examine our futures together. We may not be able to do anything about our past, but we can do absolutely anything with our future!

Jesus Christ, the reason for any legacy of any significance—I cannot thank You enough for everything You have done! You wrote our futures before the world ever was—*and You allow us to be part of Your legacy!* The only way to say "Thank You" is to accept Your offer.

SINCE 1894, Moody Publishers has been dedicated to equip and motivate people to advance the cause of Christ by publishing evangelical Christian literature and other media for all ages, around the world. Because we are a ministry of the Moody Bible Institute of Chicago, a portion of the proceeds from the sale of this book go to train the next generation of Christian leaders.

If we may serve you in any way in your spiritual journey toward understanding Christ and the Christian life, please contact us at www.moodypublishers.com.

"All Scripture is God-breathed and is useful for teaching, rebuking, correcting and training in righteousness, so that the man of God may be thoroughly equipped for every good work."
—*2 TIMOTHY 3:16, 17*

MOODY
PUBLISHERS

THE NAME YOU CAN TRUST

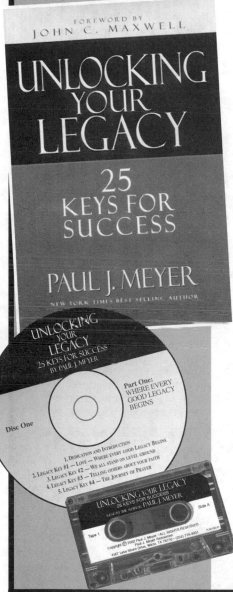

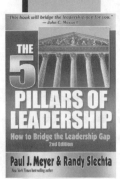
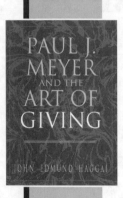